AN EXECUTIVE BRIEFING ON

Crisis Leadership

Published by the Batten Institute at the
Darden Graduate School of Business Administration
P.O. Box 6550, Charlottesville, VA 22906-6550

For distribution information contact Darden Business Publishing:
Web site: www.dardenpublishing.com
E-mail: sales@dardenpublishing.com
Phone: 800-246-3367
Fax: 434-924-4859

ISBN 1-932692-04-5

DARDEN
BUSINESS PUBLISHING
UNIVERSITY *of* VIRGINIA

Preface

Although there have long been organizations specifically designed to deal with crises, such as the military and the Red Cross, the concept of crisis management in the business community is a relatively new one. It first appeared in academic literature in the United States in the late 1970s, about the same time that businesses began to practice various crisis-management activities. Over the years, the significance of crisis management to the business community has waxed and waned, primarily as a function of economic and environmental issues. For example, the petroleum crisis of the 1970s highlighted organizational vulnerabilities and dependencies, which in turn gave rise to the growth and significance of forecasting, planning, and crisis management functions. More recently, an emphasis on crisis management has resurfaced in response to corporate fraud, widespread harassment and discrimination, and product defects and recalls. Perhaps most powerful, however, is the need for an integrated set of crisis management activities following horrific disasters such as the terrorist attacks on September 11, 2001, and Hurricane Katrina, which ravaged the gulf cost region of the United States. These and other crisis situations require that the business community, local, state, and federal agencies, and volunteer organizations work together. In our opinion, crisis management activities must be a top agenda item for leaders.

Yet despite the damage that a crisis can cause—whether it is the result of human misdeeds or natural phenomena—an organization's crisis-management activity may be more damaging to the organization than the crisis itself. In other words, leaders in organizations are underprepared for managing crisis situations and perhaps equally unprepared for preventing crises from occurring in the first place. As a result, crisis management has become synonymous with mere damage control: communication and legal strategies intended to return the organization to "normal." The notion that an organization could be better off, or positively transformed, as a result of a crisis is virtually unfathomable, and yet that is precisely the point of what we describe as crisis leadership.

This book's central message is that crisis management of old is a necessary but insufficient approach to leading organizations in an environment that is increasingly fast-paced, global, and competitive—conditions ripe for crises. Traditional crisis management has concerned itself primarily with public relations activities that help an organization scrape through potentially damaging situations with its reputation and financial standing intact. We argue that such a goal is not only shortsighted but also inadequate for remaining competitive in today's business environment. Indeed, we believe that organizations that emphasize crisis handling (before, during, and after a crisis) as a leadership issue for which all managers are responsible will perform better than organizations that relegate damage-control responsibility to the PR department Furthermore, leaders who see crises not just as threats, but as opportunities, will build stronger, more flexible organizations that become more adept at innovation and change.

The goal of this book is to expand the way managers, practitioners, and scholars think about crises, and to advance the notion that true crisis handling is a leadership issue. We came up with the idea of a book on crisis leadership during Larry Smith's Batten Fellowship at the University of Virginia's Darden School of Business. During the fellowship, we developed a program of activities and research on crisis leadership, including a two-day forum that brought together a select group of academics, public relations and crisis management practitioners, and corporate executives from the United States, Europe, and Canada. Their observations, experiences, and questions on various aspects of organizational crises and crisis leadership are the foundation for this book and the accompanying CD-ROM.

We did not coin the term *crisis leadership.* To the best of our knowledge, that distinction belongs to two prominent scholars: Ian Mitroff, the Harold Quinton Distinguished Professor of Business Policy at the Marshall School of Business at the

University of Southern California, and Christine Pearson, associate professor of management at Thunderbird, The Garvin School of International Management. Over the years, the two have jointly and independently conducted some of the earliest research on crisis leadership and have argued that crisis leadership is as much about preventing and learning from crises as it is about managing them. We were fortunate that Pearson agreed to be the keynote speaker at the forum, where she discussed crisis leadership in the context of globalization, and to contribute to this book.

The need for crisis leadership is evident when you consider the many types of crises and the damage and disruption they can inflict. The chapters in the first section of the book, "Perspectives on Crisis Leadership," speak to enhancing the likelihood that organizations not only survive but thrive in the modern-day environments that spark crises. For example, Larry Smith reviews the kinds of crises the world's businesses faced in the first half of this decade and the impact those crises had both on companies that were not prepared and on those who were. Christine Pearson contributes a chapter that asks the question, "Can you imagine?" in reference to the potential crises that exist in a global context. She argues that leaders must be mindful of unthinkable challenges, including terrorism, information warfare, and chemical and biological attacks. Erika James's chapter encourages leaders to seize the opportunity that can result when crisis management becomes crisis leadership. This chapter also presents a set of fundamental crisis-leadership competencies.

Clearly, a critical component of crisis leadership is the ability to communicate to relevant stakeholders in the midst of a crisis. Timothy Coombs's chapter presents his model of crisis communication, which is intended to help leaders develop appropriate communication strategies in response to a crisis. In a related manner, David Wooten focuses on the use of apologies as a communication strategy for managing organizational reputations.

Two chapters in the book deal explicitly with how people react to crises. Mary Waller's chapter provides a primer on panic, the fight-or-flight response to threat, and describes how panic influences leaders' ability to manage crisis situations. Garth Rowan's chapter, on the other hand, focuses on external stakeholders of organizational crises. He describes stakeholder outrage as a critical issue to be factored into any crisis-management plan.

Lynn Wooten's chapter presents a comprehensive framework for understanding and preventing organizational crises. The framework depicts effective crisis leadership as encompassing strategic design, organizational political environments, human resources management policies, and the overall organizational culture.

The second section of the book, "Crisis Leadership in Action," presents two case studies of organizations threatened by crisis situations: Cebu Pacific Air and Martha Stewart Living Omnimedia. Each case is followed by commentary that helps readers assess how the crises were handled—what worked and what could have been done differently—and how the concepts presented in earlier chapters can inform these real-life examples.

We are grateful to many people who have helped bring this project to fruition. First, we are absolutely indebted to all of the authors. Their wisdom and willingness to share their expertise are the heart of this book. We are deeply grateful to Elizabeth O'Halloran and Debbie Fisher of the Batten Institute for providing the financial and human capital, and other resources to develop our ideas. Amy Halliday was absolutely instrumental in the completion of this book. Her editing expertise helped polish each author's contribution and created a logical and coherent flow for the chapters. Gerry Yemen, senior case writer for the leadership and organizational behavior area at The Darden School, was invaluable in all aspects of the project. Her tenacity and competence were incredible assets at the conference and in the completion of this book and the CD-ROM. We also appreciate the assistance of Sara Prince, a graduate student at The Darden School, who conducted interviews with our crisis leadership experts. We respectfully acknowledge the world-class Instructional Technology Group at The Darden School, whose talent, dedication, and expertise are undeniable. In particular, we were fortunate to have had Christina Seale, Judy Jordan, and Gary Peters develop the CD-ROM. We also thank Richard Montoya, our graphic designer, for his creativity and patience. Finally, Steve Mendenhall, logistics manager extraordinaire, was phenomenal at keeping us all on track throughout the conference planning and book completion process. Thank you all!

Erika H. James
Associate Professor of Business Administration
The Darden School

Larry L. Smith
President, Institute for Crisis Management
Batten Fellow

Contents

The numbered icons in the margins guide the reader to clips on the CD-ROM in which speakers expand on, or provide a counterpoint to, issues that authors address at specific points in the book. Turn to the end of each chapter for a list of relevant clips.

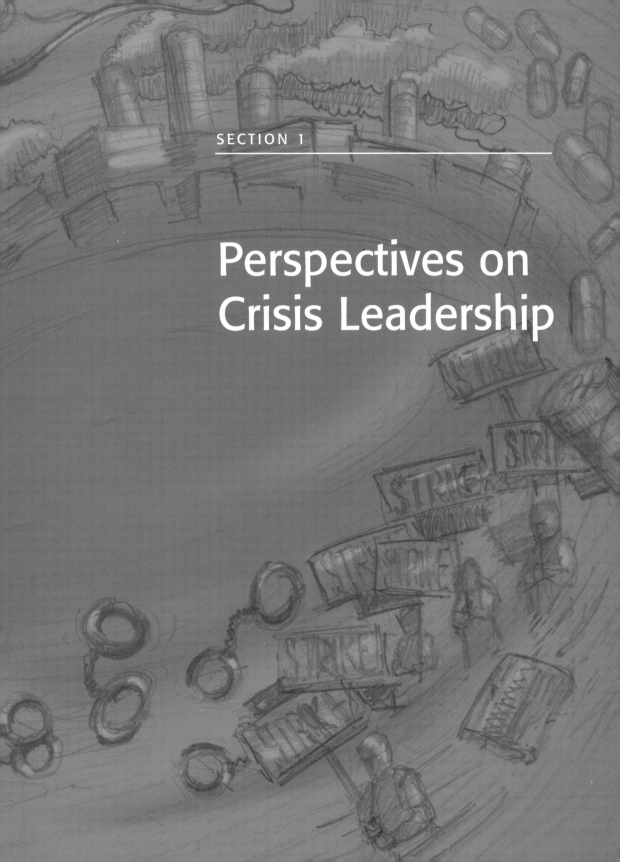

SECTION 1

Perspectives on Crisis Leadership

CHAPTER 1

Crisis Planning: From Day-to-Day Operations to the Unthinkable

Larry L. Smith is president of the Institute for Crisis Management, where he helps clients manage and prevent crises. He has over 40 years of experience in the news and public relations business. Smith started his career as a newspaper reporter and then worked as an editor, radio news reporter and anchor, news director, TV news reporter, anchor, and eventually news director of one of the top-rated news departments in the country at WHAS-TV in Louisville, Kentucky. Smith served in public information in the U.S. Air Force and later as press secretary to then-Senator Dan Quayle. He is a Batten Fellow at the University of Virginia's Darden Graduate School of Business.

by Larry L. Smith

THE FIRST HALF OF THE first decade of the new millennium saw the most crisis-filled year (2001) since the Institute for Crisis Management began tracking negative news coverage around the world. Crises such as class action lawsuits, defects and recalls, and workplace violence increased significantly that year. And who would have thought that September 11, 2001, would become a defining date in our lives? Or that just four years later another disaster, Hurricane Katrina, would devastate a famous U.S. city and force Americans to question so many things about their values and their leaders?

Vivid memories of a storm-ravaged region and flooded city, and of planes, fiery explosions, and collapsing buildings will remain with us long after we forget other events. But the attacks in New York, Pennsylvania, and at the Pentagon, and the hurricane damage in Mississippi and Louisiana were not the only crises striking companies and organizations around the globe in recent years. Many other happenings, perhaps hidden behind the flooding and dust clouds for most of us, also changed lives forever.

The downturn in the economy, the collapse of the dot-com industry, contaminated foods, tire defects, recalls in aircraft, automotive, and pharmaceutical industries, strikes or the threat of strikes in the airline industry, and fraud, insider trading, and embezzlement in banking and securities all contributed to an increase in the number of organizational crises in the first few years of the new century.

At the Institute for Crisis Management (ICM), we have compiled a crisis database by tracking business crisis news stories as reported in more than 1,500 business newspapers, magazines, wire services, and newsletters worldwide since 1990. Our database contains more than 104,000 original reports of organizations in crisis.

At ICM, we define a business crisis as any problem or disruption that triggers negative stakeholder reactions that may damage an organization's business and financial strength. We track 16 broad crisis categories:

- Catastrophes
- Environmental
- Class action lawsuits
- Consumerism actions
- Defects and recalls
- Discrimination
- Executive dismissal
- Financial damage
- Hostile takeovers
- Labor disputes
- Mismanagement
- Sexual harassment
- Whistle-blowing
- White-collar crime
- Workplace violence
- Casualty accidents

Of course, the causes and types of crises affecting corporations, large and small, vary. We have found, however, that business crises most frequently involve class action lawsuits, mismanagement, and white-collar crime. And according to our data, more situations are triggered by management than by employees or outside forces. The news coverage of such events has increased significantly over the past ten years, as one can see in the chart on the following page. This chart is not comprehensive but is a representative sampling of the crises that business news editors determined were of interest to their readers from 1994 to 2003.

So what does all this mean for business leaders as they think strategically about their companies? Bad things can happen to good companies, but it's the really good companies—those that prepare themselves ahead of time—that recover more quickly. An important step in planning for crises is understanding the different types of crises and how they have unfolded in organizations.

Crisis News Index 1994-2003

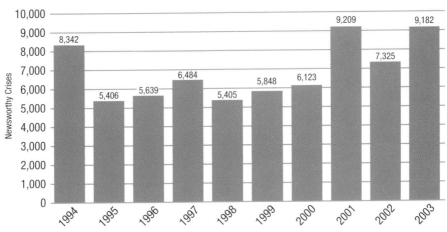

Source: Institute for Crisis Management

Smoldering or Sudden?

Most people, when they consider crisis management and planning, think about fires, explosions, natural disasters, workplace violence, and even terrorism. Yet according to ICM's crisis database, you and others in your company are far more likely to experience what we at ICM describe as a "smoldering" crisis than a "sudden" one. On average, 71 percent of all crises in the business world start out small and take days, weeks, or even months to spiral out of control and draw public attention. These are smoldering crises. In such instances, someone is aware that there may be a problem long before the crisis hits the newspapers, television, and the Internet. Smoldering crises frequently start out as small, internal problems, become public to stakeholders, and, over time, escalate to crisis status as a result of management inattention.

One example is workplace discrimination cases, which increased in 2003 and 2004 and plagued two stalwarts of Main Street, USA. At Wal-Mart, a group of former and current female employees accused the company of discriminating against them in pay and promotions. At the same time, six former and current employees of The Home Depot filed a federal lawsuit accusing the company of discriminating against them because they are African-American.

In 1990 discrimination-related class action lawsuits amounted to only 2 percent of the negative business news coverage. In 2000, however, class action lawsuits soared to 20 percent of all negative news coverage for the year. Since then, the prevalence of such lawsuits has dropped; in 2003 and 2004, they accounted for only 10 percent and 13 percent of negative news stories, respectively.

Yet other types of class action lawsuits persist. In 1990 this type of smoldering crisis amounted to only 2 percent of the negative business news coverage. In 2000, class action lawsuits soared to 20 percent of all negative news coverage for the year, dropping back to 10 percent in 2003 and 13 percent in 2004. Hundreds of thousands of consumers were included in a suit claiming that AOL had double-billed them. IBM was the subject of lawsuits in Texas and California alleging that the company knew its computer drives were defective. Consumer groups also sued Nextel and Cingular Wireless. Sony PlayStation 2 is defective according to one class action lawsuit, and in California, a doctor won a $31 million suit against UnumProvident. Another 2,500 plaintiffs are also going after the nation's largest disability insurer.

An important challenge of these and other types of smoldering crises is that they represent significant time, effort, and costs that draw resources away from a company's ability to do business. Damage awards are often higher than the actual harm and generally add up to an admission of guilt in the public eye.

Product defects and recalls, another type of smoldering crisis, were up in 2002 and 2003, representing 13 percent and 14 percent of all crises that attracted major media attention. They dropped back to a more typical 6 percent in 2004. In 2003, at least six major car companies, including Ford, Chrysler/Jeep, Nissan, Honda, General Motors, and Mercedes-Benz, recalled millions of vehicles. In 2004 General Tire and Bridgestone recalled thousands of tires. A furniture company recalled 620,000 recliners because a mechanism in the foot rest could pinch fingers. Another company recalled 8,200 extension cords that could overheat. GlaxoSmithKline recalled three Canadian asthma drugs, and counterfeit versions of Lipitor were on a recall list. A toy company recalled 126,000 toy cars, trucks, and wagons because small parts could break loose.

As consumers, we expect product perfection, but defects do occur—discount stores are full of seconds. Still, the companies mentioned above and their recalls made front-page news—why? Someone knew the engineering or manufacturing process had gone awry; why wasn't the issue addressed before it made it into our crisis news coverage database? This is the question one must ask of all smoldering crises.

Labor disputes, which tend to occur cyclically, frequently land among the top three types of crises reported by the news media and serve as another example of smoldering crises. General Electric and Coca-Cola were among the largest companies dealing with labor issues in 2003. The Coke bottling company of

Southern California fired a driver for drinking a Pepsi on duty. The Teamsters, which represent the drivers, went on the offensive, drawing massive media attention to the case. GE experienced a two-day strike in January 2005 over increases in health insurance co-payments just as the 14,000 unionized workers' three-year contract was due to expire in June. GE had 13 unions to work with and managed to avoid a protracted walkout. But the rhetoric was harsh, and the company was the center of extended media attention throughout much of the first half of the year.

If one can argue that some crises are easier to deal with than others, smoldering crises might just fit in that category. Because smoldering crises start small, organizations that are on the lookout for them have the opportunity to defuse the situation internally before it becomes public and results in extended negative news coverage, which can damage a company's reputation and whittle away at employees' morale. In the case of sudden crises—those that strike an organization out of the blue—an organization generally cannot respond out of the public eye.

On average, sudden crises, such as fires, explosions, and natural disasters, account for only 29 percent of all business crises annually. In 2003, an unexpected upward shift was due to an increase in the number of casualty accidents in the workplace. There were 664 workplace incidents that involved death or significant injuries during the year. One of the worst was a dust explosion in an automobile parts plant in Corbin, Kentucky, that killed seven workers and injured 37 others. A month earlier, an explosion of fine powder used in the manufacture of rubber medical products tore through a West Pharmaceutical Services plant in Kinston, North Carolina, killing six and injuring dozens.

In both cases, investigators ultimately found problems in the plants that, if fixed, could have prevented the disasters. Dust buildup in one plant was determined to be the cause of the deadly explosion, and investigators said it should have been recognized and eliminated. This sudden catastrophe was actually a smoldering crisis of which no one was aware. But many unexpected events occur over which an organization has virtually no control and is therefore not blamed. Indeed, there may be an initial outpouring of public support for organizations struck by a sudden crisis that was beyond management's control. Although one can prepare for a plant explosion or earthquake, it's impossible to predict the timing or likelihood of such events. Moreover, because corporate leadership is not seen as responsible or having played a role in the devastation, stakeholders tend to exhibit leniency toward the firm during a sudden crisis. Such empathy, however, is generally short-lived if the firm is perceived to be mishandling the crisis response.

One of the biggest sudden crises of 2003 was actually what we call someone else's crisis—that is, a crisis that occurs in one organization or in one place but has consequences that spill over organizational or geographic boundaries. At 4:14 P.M. on August 14, power surges knocked out electric service to 50 million people from Ohio to Ontario and Michigan to New York. Residents and businesses were without power for up to three days. New York City was blanketed in darkness, and electric trains and subways rolled to a halt. Business and industry in eight states and a significant part of Canada came to a sudden stop. Companies from grocery stores and gas stations to banks, automotive plants, and all kinds of other manufacturing facilities were unable to operate because FirstEnergy Corp. of Ohio triggered a massive rolling blackout. Detroit Edison, a subsidiary of DTE Energy, was out $16 million on costs associated with the blackout, including equipment repairs and overtime. In addition, Detroit Edison lost $14 million because it could not provide power to its customers.

Another case of "someone else's crisis" was Severe Acute Respiratory Syndrome (SARS), an epidemic that began in Asia in February 2003 and within weeks had reportedly shown up in 25 countries, including Canada. In each city where SARS was detected, it tested the strength of many businesses and industries. Tourism and the airline industries were the hardest hit as many individuals and firms cancelled trips to China, Hong Kong, and Canada.

Outside forces triggered only 19 percent of crises in the last decade. More commonly, the crises that strike corporations, large and small, are caused by management. Fifty-three percent, or more than half of all crises, are triggered by management, compared with the 28 percent that are caused by employees. For 2004, mismanagement accounted for 14 percent of all negative news coverage, and white-collar crime totaled 17 percent.

The Top Ten Lists

The Institute for Crisis Management has been compiling lists of the ten most crisis-prone industries and companies since 1990. Looking at the first half of this decade, we can only conclude that the more things change, the more they remain the same.

Telecommunications dropped from the number one spot on the top ten list in 2002, after ranking fourth in 2001, first in 2000, fourth in 1999, and ninth in 1995. Accounting and audit services made the top ten in 2003, after making headlines throughout the second half of 2002 as a victim of the corporate scandals. Electric power generating appeared on the top ten list for the first time in 2002. It dropped from eighth to tenth place in 2003. By 2004, the lists of crisis-prone industries and businesses included some veterans and some newcomers.

Even the most successful industries and companies can be quite vulnerable to

Most Crisis-Prone Industries in 2004

1. Pharmaceuticals	6. Gas/oil extraction
2. Software	7. Telecommunications
3. Insurance	8. Supermarkets
4. Airlines	9. Banking
5. Health services	10. Auto manufacturing

Ranked by percentage of ICM database

Most Crisis-Prone Companies in 2004

1. Merck	6. Parmalat SpA
2. Wal-Mart	7. Boeing
3. Enron	8. Computer Associates
4. SBC Communications	9. HealthSouth Corporation
5. Microsoft	10. Chiron Corporation

Ranked by number of ICM database records

crises. In fact, success may actually increase vulnerability. And no matter how much you try to put a decent spin on a bad press story, you have a problem. Companies in crisis need to lie low, figure out the facts, and try to stay off the front pages. This is not an easy feat, and many executives have clearly failed in the attempt. The newspapers and other media were full of stories covering the fallout of the 2002 corporate meltdown as it continued to plague the corporate world in 2003 and 2004. In the first half of the decade, the government went after the nation's fourth-largest local phone company, charging eight former and current executives with criminal and civil fraud. Martha Stewart continued to keep the public focus on her criminal and civil securities fraud, guaranteeing ongoing negative news coverage for her and her company.

A year after the Enron and WorldCom scandals, the public was still unwilling to trust corporate executives. According to a 2004 Golin Harris International survey, 69 percent of respondents said they "strongly agree" or "somewhat agree" that they don't know whom to trust. Business experts compared the corporate meltdown to a businessperson's Watergate, and some suggested that CEOs and CFOs would never experience the level of trust their predecessors did. *BusinessWeek* dubbed 2003 the time when "the New Normal began."[1] After the corporate meltdown of the year before, "many executives realized that their jobs would never be the same again. There would be more scrutiny and skepticism and even their successes would be met with less adulation." But as the magazine noted, there would be some who didn't get the "New Normal."

As many businesspeople worked hard to try to restore corporate trust, they were set back with another round of scandals, including the unraveling of health care provider HealthSouth. Drug maker Bristol-Myers Squibb was caught in accounting shenanigans and had to restate financials dating back to 1997. Dutch supermarket giant Royal Ahold, the third-largest supermarket operating in the United States, admitted to inflating profits by $500 million during the preceding two years. But it wasn't all about accounting: two former Tyson Foods managers were sentenced to one year of probation following a six-week trial in an immigration smuggling case.

Much of the nation was shocked by 2003's revelations of preferential treatment and self-dealing in the once conservative and highly respected mutual fund industry. Before the year ended, the 40-year-old former vice chair of Fred Alger & Co. became the first mutual fund executive to be sentenced to jail. Richard Strong admitted to short-term trading of his own company's mutual funds in violation of the funds' rules. He resigned and promised to repay investors for their losses. A subsidiary of bank holding company PNC Financial Services Group agreed to pay $1.15 billion to avoid a criminal trial on charges of securities violations. Investment bankers, who were once seen as smart risk takers, got a new poster boy in 2003: Frank Quattrone, who was indicted on charges of witness tampering and obstructing federal investigators.

From Running Your Business to Running Your Crisis

Arguably the biggest challenges business leaders face are low public opinion and the loss of public trust. When major newspapers print front-page timelines on corporate scandals, the perception is that business is in crisis. But what does this mean for most of us? At the very least, every organization should have a process in place to spot and fix smoldering issues before they become major problems. Paying attention to your business and those who work for you are a must. The little things matter.

Even with vigilance, however, sudden crises can strike. This means that every organization should have three crisis plans: a crisis operations plan that lays out how business is going to continue while in crisis, a crisis communication plan to prevent a mix-up over who the company spokesperson is and the key audiences to which messages must be delivered, and a business recovery plan to organize goals and targets while under duress. Ideally, these three plans should be integrated and seamless, and key executives and managers should exercise the plans at least annually and preferably twice a year.

Hundreds of businesses were wiped out as a result of Hurricane Katrina and the terrorist attacks on the World Trade Center in New York City. Those that survived did so because they anticipated the worst possible crisis. Many more did not recover because they were unprepared and lacked the leadership and foresight to weather the expected, as well as the unexpected.

In the aftermath of a crisis, executives must be able to learn from the experience. A debrief and review following any crisis provides a window of opportunity for self-reflection, which can allow the organization to gain something valuable from the situation.

A deep understanding of the issues discussed in the chapters that follow may well make the difference between defusing or inflaming difficult situations. Managing an organization in crisis is what most capable executives do well. Leading an organization through a crisis is reserved for the exceptional people who anticipate, plan, and execute before the situation gets out of control.

---

1. "The Best and Worst Manager of the Year," *BusinessWeek*, January 12, 2004.

On the CD-ROM

1. See *Biggest Challenges Organizations Face Today,* Kathleen Sutcliffe, "Economy and Workforce."

2. See *Learning to Be a Crisis Leader,* Bill McCloskey, "Examine Your Business."

3. See *Biggest Challenges Organizations Face Today,* Christophe Roux-Dufort, "Consumers and Media."

CHAPTER 2

Leading Through Crises: Twenty-First-Century, Global Challenges

Christine M. Pearson is an associate professor of management at Thunderbird, The Garvin School of International Management in Glendale, Arizona. Her research, which has been cited in more than 400 newspapers and magazines, focuses on strategic planning, leadership and organizational behavior in crisis situations, and workplace incivility, aggression, and violence. Her publications have appeared in numerous academic journals, and she is currently writing her fourth book, International Handbook of Organizational Crisis Management *(forthcoming from Sage).*

by Christine M. Pearson

O RGANIZATIONAL CRISIS MANAGEMENT as a discipline has a short history, dating back just a few decades. Some aspects of effective crisis management have not changed during that time. For instance, the objective is still to make good decisions and take actions when pressed by time and plagued by uncertainty and incomplete information. And in the decades since the discipline emerged, the basic tenets have endured: take responsibility when you are at fault, make crisis management an ongoing process, build positive relationships with key stakeholders in advance of any crisis, communicate honestly and clearly during a crisis, and take time to learn after the crisis has passed.

But although organizational crisis management has not changed in theory, it has in practice. And in the face of new kinds of threats and the unprecedented challenges of the global business environment, organizational leaders must change not only how they respond to crises but also how they think about them.

Evolving Practices

Although the guidelines for effective organizational crisis management existed decades ago, few firms put them into action. Even in the largest, most profitable organizations, crisis preparations were often limited to meeting legal requirements (by, for example, creating response plans for natural disasters or fires). Many executives considered crisis management an unnecessary form of insurance that was needed only in response to an actual incident. Rather than thinking about and preparing for potential crises, many organizations waited for the event to occur and then spent considerable resources and effort trying to hide their mistakes, keep the media at bay, and fend off employees' requests for information.

Today, despite media accounts of firms that continue to violate the principles of crisis management, many organizations have learned the value of telling the truth and telling it quickly. Whereas messengers of bad news once risked their jobs when they reported errors, today's leaders seem to value receiving timely information, even if it is negative. And although "no comment" was once a pat answer to reporters' inquiries about the sordid details of organizational crises, now effective spokespeople respect the need to share the truth, perhaps because they know that information technologies will bare it quickly anyway.

Many organizations have also improved their efforts to keep stakeholders informed. Even a decade ago, employees were often among the last to be told about crises. In the worst cases, they had to learn the latest details of their organizations' troubles from the evening news. Mindful companies today seem to have made great strides in keeping their employees informed before, during, and after a crisis or a near miss. As a result, employees are better able to provide solutions to some of the problems that arise. There have also been improvements in the speed and specificity with which organizations inform their customers when a crisis looms. Although some of these improvements can be attributed to tighter regulation and the threat of litigation, they are nonetheless impressive. But they are not enough. Effectively managing the types of crises that organizations face in the twenty-first century will require additional shifts in thinking and action.

A New Crisis Genus

To prepare for the array of crises that could affect their organizations, many savvy leaders begin by discussing the types of crises that concern them. Typically, they start with events that could devastate the core technology of their businesses. For example, bankers plan for information loss, airline executives focus on responses to aircraft accidents, manufacturers prepare for devastating product defects, and so forth. When the discussion moves beyond such core threats, similar types of crises tend to emerge across industries: bankruptcy, product or service tampering, hostile takeovers, rumors, lawsuits, and negatively sensationalized media attention, to name a few. However, the number and variety of items on these lists increased suddenly and dramatically following September 11, 2001. Since then, additional crises and their inherent challenges represent what we might consider a new "type" of crisis or, more accurately, a whole new genus. The charge of organizational leaders has changed from managing potential threats within the realm of their businesses to managing threats outside their businesses' core technologies.

Today's lists of crises are long and astoundingly complex. Crisis management discussions among mindful global business leaders include their organizations' vulnerabilities to terrorism, information warfare, chemical and biological attacks, religious extremism, and regional instability. Although these threats themselves are not new, they are newly positioned in the consciousness of many executives. To remain vigilant, executives are contemplating novel and jarring scenarios.

Can you imagine? Organizational crisis-management experts have long argued the need for mindfulness. They have cautioned leaders to be aware that success, if it breeds a "top dog" blindness about the business environment, can be a liability, and they have urged leaders to encourage diversity of perspectives, to see more and to simplify less.[1] To achieve such mindfulness, leaders are advised to foster a culture in which people feel safe questioning assumptions and reporting failures. They are urged to establish an environment in which knowledge about systems is transparent and widely known, in which people are able to redirect their focus quickly to the unexpected. Some crisis-management experts have even gone so far as to suggest that employees embrace their mistakes (to increase opportunities for learning), seek out bad news while remaining suspicious about good news (to expose problems early), and develop skepticism (to quickly recognize warning signs). All these prescriptions can enhance organizational readiness and responsiveness. But they may be insufficient in the face of the perversities that characterize twenty-first-century crises.

Perhaps the most important crisis-management question for leaders today is,

Can you imagine? This question reflects a recurring theme of *The 9/11 Commission Report*: there is danger in the lack of imagination.[2] The commission found that concerns about threatening prospects raised by the intelligence community were dismissed quickly by bureaucrats because they were deemed "too much of a distraction" and "too unrealistic."[3] Rather than thinking about the potential importance of remote signals, people "continued to react to specific, credible threats…[without performing] broader warning functions."[4] As poignantly demonstrated on September 11, when the unthinkable is dismissed without further consideration, the preemptive power of imagination is unplugged. On the basis of its extensive study, the commission concluded that "it is crucial to find a way of routinizing, even bureaucratizing, the exercise of the imagination."[5] This prescription holds true not just for government officials but also for executives in all kinds of organizations.

Effective crisis management today begins with an unconstrained imagination. Those who practice crisis management turn business assumptions on their heads by asking "what if" questions about the most dreaded, unthinkable contingencies: What if the company's own family of employees recklessly attacks the company? What if an entire population decries the company's behaviors despite its "ethical" traditions? What if company leaders line their own pockets instead of maximizing corporate profits? What if the company's most loyal and profitable customers suddenly end the relationship? Considering scenarios that overturn essential assumptions about the organization's key stakeholders, settings, and offerings requires the agility of imagination. Today's business environment requires no less. One place to start is by contemplating how global business links may compound crisis management challenges.

The Challenge of Globalization

To torque any traditional crisis-management planning and preparation, think global. Global connectedness can strain organizations and increase their vulnerability. By tapping markets, gleaning supplies, providing resources, and gaining visibility globally, weak links (that is, organizational sites that are especially vulnerable to crises) can amass exponentially. The sheer reach of a global organization's words and deeds can increase its vulnerability.

As organizations cross international boundaries, emergent chains of connections increase the likelihood of weak links. Consider a manufacturer with production facilities on several different continents. Undetected, unreported, or unresolved sabotage at one site could cause a chain effect, for example, by closing production at other sites sourced by the sabotaged product, or by contaminating supply chains. With geographic expansion, the sheer number of contacts and stakeholders grows and potential differences among them intensify the ways in which any weak or harmful link can jeopardize the entire organization. Keys to understanding and securing this vulnerability can be found in social-political, technological-structural, and psychological perspectives of crisis management.[6]

According to the social-political framework, crises occur when shared assumptions (which previously served the organization well) are jarred by the reality of a situation or an event.[7] When a disruptive event overturns an organization's assumptions about the world, the result can be a breakdown in collective sense making, and the loss of a shared sense of reality, shared beliefs, or shared values can actually trigger a crisis. For example, when a crisis looms, the interpretation of the word *crisis* can vary dramatically from one global context to another. Whereas workers in one setting may respond to a crisis alert as a top priority, those in another geographic setting may share a culture that is much less responsive to warnings. Suppose a product defect notice has been distributed to two plants with these value differences. One plant may stop production immediately and recall all distributed products, while another may make only minor adjustments to the batches that are currently in process. In the context of globalization, the seeds of crises may be sown if organizations miss or ignore these types of essential differences in values and ideologies as they cross borders.

Differing assumptions about the roles of key stakeholders and the responsibilities of the organization may exacerbate disparities across borders. Whereas government surveillance and intervention may be accepted and expected at one site, government practices in another organizational setting may keep bureaucrats out of business matters. Similarly, in one region, local media may take an aggressive approach toward questionable business news, while elsewhere even dangerous business practices may escape local media coverage. As organizations cross geographic boundaries, it becomes more difficult to establish and maintain shared objectives and practices. When shared values and beliefs are missing in a global organization, its crisis vulnerability increases because decisions and actions are unpredictable and inconsistent.

From a technological-structural perspective, organizational crises occur when tools, machines, policies, practices, routines, and leadership interact in devastating and unexpected ways.[8] When a crisis occurs in a global context, it can quickly and dramatically test the organization's technological and structural resources, including its ability to access information about what has happened internally, overcome the effects of distances between organizational sites, and secure accurate data about the external context. Something as basic as time zone differences can affect when and how people convey and receive crucial information. Unresolved variances in technologies, equipment, or policies can wreak havoc when instructions for crisis response are dispersed globally. Even procedures for accessing currency, including any foreign controls regarding its distribution, can significantly impair crisis efforts across borders. From this perspective, the variables of global business make it more difficult technologically and structurally to detect, measure, analyze, and correct crisis conditions.

Those who adopt a psychological perspective of organizational crisis management focus on the ways in which behaviors, commitments, expectations, and cognitive limitations of individuals contribute to errors in information processing and decision making, which can create crises.[9] The likelihood of such errors increases in a global organization, in which leaders must deal with language differences and sort through many possible interpretations of employees' thoughts and actions. The recognition of individual differences is crucial for crisis management. In some settings, people may expect to prepare for crises; in others, they may fervently resist, believing, for example, that such efforts will simply tempt the heavy hand of fate. Even if preparation is acceptable, people may differ in their willingness or desire to tell the truth, report bad news, or admit fault. Such individual differences can weaken the quality and speed of decisions and actions, and hinder information access. If global leaders assume that all employees will act like those closest to headquarters, their crisis-management effectiveness will be impaired.

Each of these views provides insight into the ways in which globalization increases the challenges of crisis management. Fundamentally, in a global context, there are more issues to confront, as well as more variance across and within them. Whether reflected by diversity in social values (social-political perspective), in tools, equipment, policies, and procedures (technological-structural perspective), or in individual behaviors, orientations, and limitations (psychological perspective), the difficulty of crisis management escalates in a global environment.

What's a Global Twenty-First-Century Leader to Do?

Faced with the prospect of stretching the organization's imagination and rising to the challenges of a global business arena, what is a leader to do? How can leaders build the foresight and agility they need to prepare for a new array of threats, and respond when those threats are expanded globally? The following recommendations are offered as preliminary guidelines.

Make the importance of crisis management highly visible across borders. To be effective, crisis management must be embraced and practiced consistently throughout the organization. Whether in corporate, domestic, or international operations, organizational members must recognize that a threat anywhere in the firm can put the whole organization at risk. Leaders must emphasize the relevance of crisis preparation across cultures and hold employees accountable, regardless of their locations. Where values collide, differences must be overcome. But differences may have a silver lining: the variance that can beget crises can also enhance imagination by fostering depth and breadth of ideas and actions.

Demonstrate crisis management values in the organization's actions, regardless of the setting. Despite economic, social, cultural, or political differences across organizational sites, leaders must always do the right thing. This is good business practice domestically and essential business practice globally. Although wrongful actions taken in remote organizational locations might seem like they will elude the eye of the public, they will not.

Recognize, value, and adapt to diverse attitudes and behaviors across borders. To forestall crises in distant sites, guard against corporate-headquarters-as-the-center-of-the-universe thinking. Emphasize global over corporate in crisis management communications and actions. To improve organizational imagination about crises, embrace diversity in global crisis preparations.

Facilitate cross-cultural representation. Crisis management training must include foreign operations. The crisis management team should include members from key international sites. And when crises or near misses occur, best practices should be communicated clearly and honestly across all settings. Imaginative thinking is enhanced when cross-cultural representatives have a voice.

Build stakeholder bonds across borders. When a crisis hits, the individuals, groups, and organizations that influence or are influenced by the organization become critical to its survival. All too often, fragile networks disintegrate as those affiliated with the organization attempt to distance themselves. Building strong bonds across borders in advance of any crisis, and investing in "what if" thinking with new stakeholders, increases the parameters of imagined futures and facilitates ad hoc access to resources when a crisis occurs.

Manage and translate information carefully. When an organization operates across international borders, understanding the access, reach, and strength of various communication media is a complex challenge. The better the organization understands and works with diverse media outlets in advance of a crisis, the faster and more effectively it can channel information during a crisis. Broad, multimedia approaches increase transparency across borders. Simple, consistent messages around the world enhance clarity.

No leaders can prepare their organizations for every bizarre event that might cause harm, nor should they. But being among today's best-prepared global organizations does require a new mode of thinking, openness, and transparency. As new forms of crises and the additional challenges of globalization interact, so, too, do the organization's resources for contemplating, preparing for, and resolving those crises. When organizations invest in the effort to integrate global perspectives—by listening to culturally diverse stakeholders—and to gather disparate resources—by gaining commitments from geographically dispersed sites—the solution can actually lie in the problem. Imagine that.

---

1. I.I. Mitroff and C.M. Pearson, *Crisis Management* (San Francisco: Jossey-Bass, 1993); K. Weick and K. Sutcliffe, *Managing the Unexpected: Assuring High Performance in an Age of Complexity* (San Francisco: Jossey-Bass, 2001).

2. National Commission on Terrorist Acts, *The 9/11 Commission Report: Final Report of the National Commission on Terrorist Acts Upon the United States* (NY: W.W. Norton & Company, 2004).

3. Ibid., p. 346.

4. Ibid., p. 347.

5. Ibid., p. 344.

6. For further discussion of these perspectives, see C. Pearson and J. Clair, "Reframing Crisis Management," *Academy of Management Review* 23 (1998): 59-76.

7. See, for example, B. Turner, "The Organizational and Interorganizational Development of Disasters," *Administrative Science Quarterly* 21 (1976): 378-397.

8. See, for example, C. Perrow, *Normal Accidents: Living with High-Risk Technologies* (NY: Basic Books, 1984).

9. K. Weick, "Enacted Sensemaking in Crisis Situations," *Journal of Management Studies* 25 (1988): 305-317.

On the CD-ROM

1. See *Learning to Be a Crisis Leader,* Christophe Roux-Dufort, "Integrate Crisis Management and Core Business."

2. See *Creating a Crisis Leadership Culture,* Kathleen Sutcliffe, "Develop a Mindful Organization."

3. See *Biggest Challenges Organizations Face Today,* Kathleen Sutcliffe, "Global and Local."

4. See *Creating a Crisis Leadership Culture,* Ron Culp, "Could This Happen Here?"

5. See *Biggest Challenges Organizations Face Today,* Ron Culp, "Credibility."

CHAPTER 3

Leadership in an Era of Crisis and Opportunity

by Erika H. James

Erika H. James is an associate professor of business administration at the University of Virginia's Darden School of Business, where she teaches organizational behavior. She conducts research in the areas of crisis leadership and workforce diversity. Her most recent work focuses on crises as a source of organizational innovation and change, and crisis response strategies for managing discrimination lawsuits. James's research has been published or is forthcoming in several leading academic journals, including Academy of Management Journal, Strategic Management Journal, Organization Science, *and* Journal of Applied Psychology.

PICTURE THIS SCENARIO: A reporter confronts you as you stroll to your car at the end of a long day. She shoves a microphone in your face while the glare of the video camera temporarily blinds you. All you hear is, "Excuse me, Mr. CEO, how do you respond to the widespread allegations of sexual harassment by senior executives in your company?" You are caught completely off guard, yet clearly you are expected to say (and do) something.

Now picture this: You have just returned to your office and see the voice-mail light flashing on your telephone. To your horror, you are listening to a message from one of your direct reports describing one reported death and numerous injuries to children as a result of a malfunction in your top-selling children's product. The next message is from your firm's legal counsel suggesting that the firm prepare itself for a long court battle.

Or imagine that things have been running smoothly in the chemical plant you manage. It has been six months since an accident report has been filed, and you are confident that your efforts to establish a safety culture are finally paying off. That is, until today, when a chemical spill caused an explosion at the plant. As a result, toxic material is leaking into the environment.

In recent years, crisis situations like these have become all too familiar to many, albeit still a minority of, executives. The consequences of mishandling crises for a firm's reputation can linger. I want to emphasize that it is often the handling—or, rather, mishandling—of a crisis, not the crisis itself, that can have the most extreme consequences, positive and negative. I also want to emphasize in this chapter that effective leadership during a crisis spells the difference between organizations that are done in by a negative event and those that not only survive a crisis but perhaps even grow stronger as a result. Below are just a few ways in which crises affect organizations.

Crisis Consequences

From least to most severe, the consequences of a crisis are damage to a company's reputation, its financial well-being, and its survival. These consequences often occur sequentially. A threat to a company's reputation, for example, can trigger a decline in consumer confidence that, in turn, can threaten a firm's financial standing. And a company whose financial performance declines for too long will not survive.

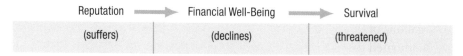

Reputation	Financial Well-Being	Survival
(suffers)	(declines)	(threatened)

Reputation. As Benjamin Franklin once said, "Glass, china, and reputation are easily cracked, and never mended well." People and organizations whose reputations have been damaged will likely have a profound appreciation for Franklin's insight. But what exactly is a corporate reputation, and why is it important?

Reputation means different things to different kinds of stakeholders. From a strategist's perspective, reputation is an asset that can contribute to a firm's competitive advantage in the marketplace and therefore must be managed.[1] Marketing experts tend to take a somewhat different approach by focusing on how a firm's product and service brands can help build corporate reputation.[2] Corporate communication and public relations specialists see reputation as an important component in crisis management and in the development of a firm's overall image.[3] Lastly, corporate reputation has received a great deal of attention in the popular press, which has led to publications such as *Fortune* magazine's "Most Admired Corporations." When considering a firm's reputation, the media tend to focus on the performance indicators that inform investors.[4]

The cornerstone of reputation is perception, or the way people view the organization. These perceptions are of course influenced by the priorities of various stakeholders. Is it, for example, the products or services a firm provides, its ability to create value for shareholders, or the responsiveness and responsibility for the communities in which it operates? Reputation is truly in the eye of the beholder. When a firm is beheld in a negative light, financial consequences will likely ensue.

Financial Well-Being. A negative corporate reputation (one resulting from a poorly managed crisis, for example) can severely threaten a firm's bottom line. Some of the more obvious examples of the costs incurred by crises include legal fees, clean-up costs, compensation to victims, and repairs. Below, I've grouped the cost of crises into categories that reflect direct recovery costs and costs associated with market decline and competition.

Direct Recovery Costs. The monetary figures associated with recovering from some crises are indeed staggering. The examples below merely represent the direct payout for some well-known organizational crises but do not include the intangibles, such as the opportunity costs of having senior leadership's time and attention focused on the crisis instead of on the business.

- March 24, 1989 marked one of the most notorious environmental disasters in the United States. The *Exxon Valdez* oil tanker spilled nearly 11 million gallons of oil into the waters of Prince William Sound. The oil spill to date is estimated to have cost the company in excess of $13 billion.
- On December 21, 1988, Pan Am flight 103, traveling from London to New York City, exploded over Lockerbie, Scotland, killing 259 passengers and crew and 11 people on the ground. The explosion cost the now defunct airline $652 million.
- As a result of improper financial reporting in the late 1990s and early 2000s, telecommunications giant WorldCom has paid out more than $750 million to investors and declared Chapter 11 bankruptcy.
- In 1996, Texaco settled a racial discrimination lawsuit for $176 million, which at the time was the largest settlement for a racial discrimination lawsuit in the U.S.

Market Reactions. The failure to address a crisis situation adequately and in a timely fashion gives stakeholders the opportunity to "fill in the blanks." In the absence of information, or in the presence of poor or inadequate information, investors tend to assume the worst and then act accordingly. When institutional investors lose confidence in a firm and its leadership during times of crisis, we often see active trading of the firm's shares and a substantial drop in share price. For example, after allegations that food from the Jack in the Box restaurant chain caused an outbreak of E. coli bacteria, the company's market value fell 75 percent. Similarly, after allegations of insider trading by Martha Stewart became public, the stock price for Martha Stewart Living Omnimedia (MSO) began a downward spiral, plunging from nearly $20 per share to just over $10 per share. More than a year later, the value of the MSO stock had not recovered.

Competitive Disadvantage. Crisis situations often mean that a company is, at least temporarily, in a weakened state, vulnerable to takeover bids or challenges from rivals. In 1999, for instance, when Coca-Cola products were linked to illness in schoolchildren in Belgium and France, stores pulled the products from their shelves. Competitors were primed to pick up the slack, taking over Coca-Cola's shelf space and threatening the firm's 49 percent market share.

In short, the total cost of many crises is difficult to quantify because so many of the costs are intangible. Beyond the direct recovery cost, loss in market share, and decline in stock price, other less easily measured costs associated with a crisis also threaten a firm's financial well-being. Legal fees, mass marketing or advertising campaigns, increases in insurance premiums, and loss of human capital may be difficult to quantify, but their impact should not be taken lightly.

Firm Survival. By now it should be clear that corporate crisis situations are serious, and while a best-case scenario for firms who have mishandled a crisis might be a short-lived slump in reputation, one cannot deny that at the other extreme is the very real possibility that the firm may not survive. In recent years, we have seen numerous examples of firms declaring bankruptcy or experiencing a loss of stakeholder trust and then, as a result, facing their demise. Does this have to be? I think not! But surviving a crisis requires an intentional effort on the part of organizational leaders to rise to the challenge that crises present.

Crisis Leadership

What differentiates firms that thrive following a crisis from those that do not is leadership. Crisis leadership is similar to what we think of as "traditional" leadership, with the following exceptions: it almost always occurs in public view and therefore is subject to more scrutiny, and it requires expedited decision making. I believe that it is important to consider the behavioral elements of crisis leadership, as distinct from leadership in more ordinary times, given the circumstances that embody crisis situations. Recently, Lynn Wooten and I identified a set of competencies that can help leaders rise to the challenges associated with running today's organizations, especially when those challenges achieve crisis status.[5]

Crisis Competency 1: Adopt an Inclusive Corporate Mindset

All too often, organizational leaders are unduly influenced by powerful (or presumably powerful) stakeholders. For publicly owned organizations, individual and institutional investors, which have certain expectations for firm performance, represent one such group. In recent years, some organizations have succumbed to the pressure these investors exert in ways that are both unethical and illegal. The pressure to reach earnings targets, for example, can lead to a short-term perspective when, in reality, both short-term and long-term considerations are important. And once leaders satisfy a particularly influential stakeholder group, and are rewarded for doing so, the pressure to keep that group happy can create a mindset that allows for risky behavior and the neglect of other stakeholders.

The challenge we pose to corporate leaders is to develop a more expansive and inclusive mindset. This may include, for example, considering the impact of business decisions on multiple stakeholders, not just those who wield power and influence. An inclusive mindset also refers to taking a big-picture perspective so that one is constantly in tune with how actions and decisions in one part of the business may have an impact on another area of the organization. By looking at the big picture, leaders can more readily appreciate their accountability to all stakeholders and may be better able to prioritize stakeholders' needs. Moreover, with an inclusive and expanded mindset, leaders may be better positioned to recognize the potential for crises before they occur and should be able to find a more effective resolution for those crises that do occur.

Crisis Competency 2: Perform Regular Vulnerability Audits

Many organizations have a crisis plan, one piece of which identifies particular vulnerabilities. All too often, however, firms have identified and planned only for obvious ways in which they may succumb to crises. A manufacturing firm planning for workplace safety or equipment malfunctions is one example of such traditional crisis "management." Crisis leadership, however, involves anticipating the less obvious scenarios, such as intentional sabotage of machinery or, worse, the use of company equipment as a weapon. Certainly a leader can never anticipate all possible crisis scenarios, but at the very least crisis leaders consider and plan for many of the obvious—and a few of the less obvious—threats.

The need to identify less obvious organizational vulnerabilities is easy to understand but difficult to implement, precisely because many of the not-so-obvious crises are brought on by people. Mismanagement, corporate fraud, and unethical behavior, although believed to be taboo, rank among the most frequently reported types of crisis situations. But leaders find it hard to imagine that anyone in their organization would engage in such behavior, much less that they themselves would. Yet, by believing in the goodness of our intentions, it becomes extraordinarily difficult to accept that our actions are anything less than above board. In fact, our minds can find ways to justify our deeds, so much so that we are genuinely disturbed when others interpret our behavior as unethical, immoral, or illegal. In short, leaders must continually challenge themselves to consider not only the possibility that undesirable situations occur in their organizations, but also that they may have played a role in creating environments where bad things happen.

Crisis Competency 3: Own the Decision Making During a Crisis

Traditional approaches to decision making involve gathering information, generating alternatives, evaluating those alternatives, and reaching a decision. During times of crisis, however, this traditional approach becomes less appropriate because it assumes unlimited information and unlimited time, both of which are generally unavailable during stressful situations. Yet during many crises, crisis handlers fail to adopt a suitable decision-making alternative. Instead, they tend to abdicate decision-making power to a select group. Corporate counsel is often first on the list, which likely explains why the most common initial communication is a denial or a "no comment." Lawyers often encourage leaders to say as little as possible or to deny allegations altogether in order to avoid or limit legal culpability. Denials are fine if in fact the firm is not guilty of any wrongdoing, but time and again we find that companies are forced to backpedal and engage in even more damage control when additional information becomes public.

The tendency to rely too much on the advice of others during a crisis is completely natural. After all, we hire specialists and experts precisely because of their knowledge base in particular areas. Leaders will often depend on expert opinion during crises to offset the uncertainty associated with crisis situations. A savvy organizational leader will recognize, however, that it is not the expert, but the leader him- or herself who has the broadest perspective on the organization and is thus best positioned to make appropriate decisions. The narrow focus of the expert is important, but only in the context of the leader's big-picture perspective.

Crisis Competency 4: Seize the Opportunity That Crises Create

Opportunity from crisis? "Impossible," you say? Well, think again. In fact, the Chinese use the same character to denote crisis and opportunity. Yet it is understandable why the two concepts would seem to be at odds. Crises threaten organizations, so we tend to believe that the most likely outcome will be negative. But under the right set of circumstances, including a leader's ability to adopt the aforementioned competencies, opportunities can materialize from crises.

Consider, for example, what happened when capsules of Johnson & Johnson's number-one-selling product, Tylenol, were laced with cyanide, resulting in eight deaths. J&J's leaders might have allowed the threat to the company, and the fear the crisis elicited, to influence their response. Oftentimes, management responses to threats such as this reflect damage control activities, including public relations campaigns and denial communication. J&J, however, considered its corporate credo as well as the perspectives of multiple stakeholders to determine a course of action that has helped position J&J as one of the most admired companies in the United States. Not only did the company's reputation benefit, but also, as a result of leadership thinking beyond the immediate terms of the crisis, the company's research and development unit developed tamper-resistant packaging that is now used throughout the pharmaceutical industry. In both of these ways, J&J was able to realize opportunity from crisis. In short, leaders who are able to frame crises as potential opportunities will likely manage organizations in a way that will make them more resilient and perhaps even better off after the crisis than the organizations of leaders who view crises only as threats.

Conclusion

In closing, crisis leadership reflects a set of competencies, some of which challenge our fundamental assumptions and natural proclivities during crisis situations. Learning and modifying behavior take time and practice. And because crisis events by definition are rare and require quick action, organizational leaders are generally unable or unwilling to devote necessary resources to develop crisis leadership skills in themselves or in others. Yet, crisis leadership, as opposed to crisis management, is precisely the ability to demonstrate the core set of behaviors identified here in a complex and dynamic environment, and to do so under a spotlight. The consequences of not building and using the repertoire of crisis leadership competencies can be significant, both personally for the leader and organizationally. Can one learn to become a crisis leader? Absolutely! Will developing crisis leadership competencies take commitment and resources? Absolutely! But the payoff can be enhanced individual and organizational reputations, as well as the creation of groundbreaking technologies or systems.

---

1. J.F. Mahon, "Corporate Reputation: A Research Agenda Using Strategy and Stakeholder Literature," *Business & Society* 44 (4) (2002): 415-445.

2. Ibid.

3. Ibid.

4. Ibid.

5. E.H. James and L.P. Wooten, "Leadership as (Un)usual: How to Display Competence in Times of Crisis," *Organizational Dynamics* 34 (2) (2005): 41-152.

On the CD-ROM

1 See *Biggest Challenges Organizations Face Today,* David Shapiro, "Regulators and Litigation."

2 See *Crisis Management vs. Crisis Leadership,* all speakers.

3 See *Learning to Be a Crisis Leader,* Bill McCloskey, "Be Open to Hearing Information."

4 See *Creating a Crisis Leadership Culture,* Ron Culp, "Allow Time for Open Exchange."

5 See *Learning to Be a Crisis Leader,* Christophe Roux-Dufort, "Acknowledge Problems."

6 See B*iggest Challenges Organizations Face Today,* Kathleen Sutcliffe, "Threats or Opportunities."

CHAPTER 4

Applying Situational Crisis Communication Theory

W. Timothy Coombs is an associate professor in the department of communication studies at Eastern Illinois University in Charleston. His research focuses on the development and testing of Situational Crisis Communication Theory (SCCT). He was awarded the 2002 Jackson, Jackson and Wagner Behavioral Research Prize from the Public Relations Society of America and the 2002 PRIDE Award for Best Article from the Public Relations Division of the National Communication Associations. He is the author of Ongoing Crisis Communication and has published over 30 articles and book chapters on crisis-related topics. Coombs holds a Ph.D. in public affairs and issues management from Purdue University.

by W. Timothy Coombs

A MONG AN ORGANIZATION'S most valuable assets is its reputation. During a crisis, obviously the crisis management team's primary concern must be protecting people whose lives are threatened. But the organization's reputation may also be at risk and must be safeguarded. Post-crisis communication, what the "organization" says and does after a crisis, can go a long way toward protecting its reputation and therefore must be approached thoroughly and strategically. Situational Crisis Communication Theory (SCCT), which I developed in 1995, helps crisis managers dissect organizational crises in a way that can inform their communication strategies. One theme that emerges from communication research is that situation is a crucial consideration in crafting effective messages. SCCT's name reflects this idea, emphasizing that the nature of the crisis situation helps determine which strategies will best protect the organization's reputation. I developed the theoretical aspects of SCCT in other writings.[1] In this chapter, I focus on the application of the theory.

Assessing Reputational Threats

SCCT, and the communication strategies it suggests, is driven by the reputational threat a crisis situation presents. The reputational threat, in turn, is driven by how organizational stakeholders—any individual or group who can either affect or be affected by the organization—interpret the event and where they place blame. People naturally make attributions of responsibility for negative events.[2] Following early work in marketing that was based on attribution theory, SCCT presumes that stakeholders, including the crisis team, will work at interpreting a crisis and will reach some conclusions about who or what is responsible.[3] They may attribute the crisis to the organization itself or to external factors. The stronger the attributions of responsibility to the organization, the greater the reputational threat.[4] Of course there may be competing interpretations and finger-pointing, but usually a dominant interpretation emerges, a way in which most people are framing the event. And this dominant frame will be determined in large part by what type of crisis it is. A crucial first step, therefore, for crisis managers trying to evaluate the reputational threat posed by a crisis and develop appropriate communication strategies is to determine to which of three crisis families the situation belongs.

Victim crises are situations in which the organization suffers harm largely because of outside forces rather than its own actions. Examples include natural disasters, product tampering, workplace violence, and rumors. When an organization is clearly a victim of such events, it will assume little or no responsibility for the crisis, and its reputation will not be seriously threatened. *Accidental crises* are events that are unintentional and beyond the organization's reasonable control. Such crises, which generate low attributions of crisis responsibility, include outside challenges, technical-error accidents, and technical-error product harm. They can be thought of as the risks associated with operating the organization. For example, chemical facilities can have spills or leaks, railroads can experience derailments, and activist groups can challenge how an organization operates. *Preventable crises* occur when organizational members are perceived to have knowingly and even willingly put stakeholders at risk, perhaps in violation of the law. Such crises generate very strong attributions of responsibility and thus pose serious threats to the organization's

Crisis Types

Victim Crises

Natural Disasters:
Acts of nature, such as an earthquake, that damage an organization.

Rumors:
False and damaging information that is being circulated.

Workplace Violence:
An attack by a current or former employee on current employees on-site.

Product Tampering/Malevolence:
Damage to an organization caused by an external agent.

Accidental Crises

Challenges:
A claim by stakeholders that an organization is operating in an inappropriate manner.

Technical-Error Accidents:
A technology or equipment failure that causes an industrial accident.

Technical-Error Product Harm:
A technology or equipment failure that causes a product to be defective or potentially harmful.

Preventable Crises

Human-Error Accidents:
An industrial accident caused by human error.

Human-Error Product Harm:
A product that is defective or potentially harmful because of human error.

Organizational Misdeed:
An action that puts stakeholders at risk and/or violates the law.

reputation. Such crises include organizational misdeeds, human-error accidents (which presumably could have been prevented), and human-error product harm.

Crises are largely perceptual. Stakeholders take their cues about an event from the news media and from messages on the organization's Web site. Crisis managers must be sure to study the media's presentation of the crisis to determine what cues are being conveyed. There are times, especially if the facts are ambiguous, when the media will frame a crisis differently than the crisis team does. The team can choose either to work with the media's frame or to create a different one.

In the case of natural disasters and workplace violence, it's generally clear right away that the organization was a victim, and a shared frame will quickly emerge. Other instances, however, may not be so clear and will require the organization to participate more actively in sending cues that help stakeholders frame the event. For rumors and product tampering, for instance, the organization and possibly authorities must prove that the information is false or demonstrate evidence of tampering. Snapple, for example, amid rumors that the ship on the label of its iced tea bottle was a slave ship, was able to prove otherwise by identifying the ship as a drawing of the Boston Tea Party ship from a Bettman Archive document. Pepsi used footage of its production line to prove that a syringe could not be placed in Pepsi cans and that, therefore, the company must have been a victim of product tampering. In accidents and product harm incidents, the media generally focus on the events that transpired because causes are rarely known at first.[5] Certain groups may try to influence the frame of an accident or product harm case by blaming management, but disputes over the way such events are framed are rare. The key is to determine what crisis type is being presented to stakeholders and then use that information to determine the initial reputational threat.

Once crisis managers have identified what type of crisis occurred—and what is being communicated to stakeholders—the next step in assessing the reputational threat is to evaluate the crisis modifiers: aspects of an organization's circumstances that may influence how a crisis is perceived. Modifiers include an organization's crisis history and its performance history. Crisis leaders should prepare a crisis audit, a list of past crises, in order to assess how crisis history might affect the current crisis-management effort. Crisis history is important because the news media do report past incidents—especially similar ones—when covering a crisis. If an organization has a history of similar crises, the reputational threat will intensify with each instance. Past crises suggest a pattern of bad behavior rather than a simple miscue. Studies have yet to demonstrate empirically a beneficial effect from a positive crisis history—that is, no past crises.

Performance history—how the organization has treated stakeholders such as employees, the community, and customers—is another potential crisis modifier. Because reputation is in large part a function of an organization's interactions with its stakeholders, performance history can be thought of as prior reputation.[6] A poor performance history intensifies the reputational threat in the same way that crisis history does. Research has demonstrated that the reputation of an organization during a crisis will be viewed less favorably when the performance history of the organization is negative.[7]

It has long been assumed that a positive performance history will help protect the organization's reputation during a crisis, and there is indeed some research to support this belief.[8] Positive performance history adds reputational capital to the organization's bank account. When a crisis occurs, the organization has more reputational capital to spend. The crisis is still a threat, but the organization can absorb the damage more easily.

Because stakeholders adjust their opinions about an organization when they learn of a negative crisis history or an unfavorable performance history, crisis managers in such organizations must adjust their assessments of the reputational threat of a crisis. When a modifier is present, victim crises will have a threat level equal to accidental crises, and accidental crises will have a threat level equal to intentional, preventable crises.

Selecting the Post-Crisis Response

Once the crisis leader has assessed the reputational threat, he or she selects an appropriate post-crisis response. Various lists of response strategies have been developed by researchers in management and communication.[9] There is no one, perfect list because the value of any communication strategies depends on how they will be used. According to SCCT, crisis responsibility is a primary driver in determining the reputational threat of a crisis. Therefore, perceived acceptance of responsibility is a key factor in evaluating post-crisis responses. SCCT organizes response strategies according to how much each is perceived as the organization taking responsibility for the crisis and demonstrating concern for victims. The SCCT framework includes four postures, each of which is associated with several strategies: denial, diminishment, rebuilding, and bolstering.

Denial is the severing of any connection between the organization and the crisis. Diminishment is the attempt to reduce the attributions of organizational responsibility for the crisis and thus its negative impact. Rebuilding is a direct effort to improve the organization's reputation. Finally, bolstering is a supplemental strategy: an organization that has had positive relationships with stakeholders can draw on their goodwill to help protect the organization's reputation, perhaps by praising stakeholders or by portraying itself as a victim of the crisis and thus eliciting stakeholders' sympathy.

The four postures reflect various attitudes about the organization's responsibility for the crisis and how it treats victims. Denial assumes no responsibility and argues

SCCT Crisis Response Strategies by Posture

Denial Posture

Denial: Crisis manager asserts that there is no crisis. *The organization said there was no chemical release today—the cloud was only water vapor.*

Attack the Accuser:
Crisis manager confronts the person or group making the negative claim about the organization. *The organization threatened to sue the people who claimed it was funding the KKK.*

Scapegoat: Crisis manager blames some person or group outside of the organization for the crisis. *The organization blamed its supplier for the E. coli outbreak.*

Diminishment Posture

Excuse: Crisis manager minimizes organizational responsibility by denying any intent to do harm and/or claiming an inability to control the events that triggered the crisis. *The organization said the facility operates safely but that dust explosions can occur any time organic dust is present.*

Justification: Crisis manager minimizes the perceived damage caused by the crisis. This often involves correcting misperceptions. *The organization said the facility will reopen tomorrow because the damage was minor even though the explosion was very loud.*

Rebuilding Posture

Apology: Crisis manager indicates that the organization takes full responsibility for the crisis and asks stakeholders for forgiveness. *The organization publicly accepted full responsibility for the chemical release and asked nearby residents to forgive the mistake.*

Compensation: Crisis manager offers money or other help and support to victims. *The organization gave free hotel rooms and meal allowances to community members displaced by the chemical release.*

Bolstering Posture

Victimage: The organization makes clear to stakeholders that it is a victim of the crisis. *The organization stated that it had suffered the loss of valued employees from the tragic violence.*

Reminder: Crisis manager tells stakeholders about the past good works of the organization. *The organization restated its recent work to improve K-12 education.*

Ingratiation: Crisis manager praises stakeholders. *The organization thanked local first responders and emergency personnel for saving its facility.*

that there are no victims. Diminishment suggests some acceptance of responsibility and shows some concern for victims. Rebuilding creates strong perceptions of accepting responsibility and demonstrates a keen concern for victims. Bolstering strategies avoid any discussion of responsibility but can acknowledge the crisis. For instance, victimage—one of the bolstering strategies—acknowledges the crisis but defines the organization as a victim, thereby avoiding responsibility.

Postures Applied to Crisis Communication

The communications from an organization in the immediate aftermath of a crisis must of course be about helping victims, not about saving the organization's reputation. The organization must first give stakeholders instructing and adjusting information—that is, information about how stakeholders can protect themselves physically, by, for example, returning a contaminated product, and about how they can cope psychologically. After such essential information has been conveyed, it is time to think more strategically. Post-crisis response strategies can protect an organization's reputation by altering attributions about the crisis, changing perceptions of the organization, or through a combination of the two. In general, the denial and diminishment postures seek to shift responsibility away from the organization, while the rebuilding and bolstering postures attempt to improve perceptions of the organization. The challenge is to determine which posture and which of the associated strategies will protect or restore the organization's reputation most effectively. The more stakeholders believe that the organization is responsible for the negative events, the more important it is for the organization to communicate in a way that demonstrates an acceptance of responsibility and a concern for victims.

The denial posture is appropriate when the organization believes no crisis has occurred. If negative rumors are circulating about a company, for instance, the company can simply deny them. Reebok, for example, fought unfounded charges that it used factories in South Africa during apartheid. Denial may also be appropriate when an organization's practices are challenged. When Southern Baptists called for a boycott of Disney because the company was offering benefits for same-sex partners, the company defended its position on national television and in the print media. Before adopting the denial posture, however, crisis leaders must be confident that they can convince key stakeholders that there was no crisis and that the company is operating properly. Some companies, when challenged, change advertising or simple business practices simply to escape negative publicity. Lowe's, Tyson Foods, and Kellogg's all stopped advertising on ABC's controversial show *Desperate Housewives* because of customers' complaints, while Wendy's changed its beef-purchasing practices after PETA pressured the fast-food chain to demand that suppliers improve their treatment of animals.[10] A crisis leader must believe the fight to win the hearts and minds of key stakeholders is worth the cost. Pyrrhic victories offer little comfort or benefit to the organization.

Denial can also be an effective response to accusations that a company's products are harmful. Generally organizations do not deny and fight accusations of product harm because of the risk of alienating customers. Firestone has twice fought tire recalls only to relent. A delayed recall creates the perception that the organization does not really care about customer safety. In the 1980s, Gerber fought off charges that there were pieces of glass in jars of Gerber baby food, enlisting the FDA to prove its innocence. Gerber kept the product on the market throughout the crisis, a move that may ultimately have contributed to an erosion of the company's market share. Most organizations favor conservative approaches to product harm and often recall a product quickly, even on the basis of limited evidence.[11]

Attacking the accuser and scapegoating, both strategies associated with the denial posture, are viewed negatively by stakeholders. Unless an organization is completely uninvolved in the crisis, scapegoating should be avoided. Stakeholders react negatively when an organization that bears some responsibility for a crisis shifts blame to someone else. Odwalla quickly stopped blaming suppliers in its response to a deadly E. coli incident in the 1990s. But some damage had already been done: stakeholders reacted negatively, noting that the company initially had tried to avoid responsibility. Some consultants, such as Eric Dezenhall of Dezenhall Resources, advocate aggressive attack-the-accuser strategies any time an organization is challenged.[12] But an organization that adopts such strategies can damage its long-term relationships with stakeholders. Corporations look mean when they attack less powerful accusers such as consumer groups or someone who has created a Web site questioning the company's practices. Moreover, those challenging the organization could be customers or investors who are raising legitimate points for discussion. Crisis managers need to weigh the short-term and long-term advantages and disadvantages of an attack-the-accuser strategy.

Accidental crises call for a diminishment posture. The two strategies associated with this posture operate on different levels. The excuse strategy reminds stakeholders that the situation was beyond the organization's control—certain accidents happen in certain industries—and reinforces the organization's low level of responsibility. The justification strategy seeks to correct misperceptions of a crisis. There are times when the visual effects of a crisis, such as an explosion or a fire, or inaccurate news media presentations make a crisis appear worse than it is. The justification strategy uses facts to align perceptions of the seriousness of a crisis with the reality. When a storage tank burst in Cincinnati, for example, the news media reported a large fish kill in the Ohio River, thus representing the event as a serious environmental threat. The company attempted to correct this impression by explaining that the chemical, in fact, was nontoxic and that no fish had been harmed. Justification should be reserved for situations in which factual errors are creating inaccurate perceptions of an event. Little is gained from debating actual victims about how bad a crisis is. People who are suffering will think it is very bad regardless of what the organization says.

Preventable crises demand the rebuilding posture. The serious reputational threat must be counterbalanced and the organization's responsibility acknowledged. Rebuilding strategies are positive actions, perceived as the acceptance of responsibility for the crisis. The goal is to alter perceptions of the organization in crisis by demonstrating concern for the victims. Compensation offers victims restitution in the form of money, goods, or services. Providing housing for people displaced by an evacuation or offering them a per diem are all examples. Ashland Oil, for instance, paid for water to be shipped into communities whose water supplies had been polluted when one of the company's storage tanks ruptured. An apology is a public admission of responsibility coupled with a request for forgiveness. The downside of apologies is that they leave an organization open to financial liability.[13] In 1996, Texaco apologized for its racial discrimination practices and asked for a second chance. The company also began immediate action on lawsuits by offering settlements totaling over $140 million.

A bolstering posture is most effective in response to victim crises. Such crises are unique because both the organization and stakeholders suffer. This is especially true in the case of natural disasters, workplace violence, and product tampering. The victimage strategy can be used in conjunction with instructing and adjusting information. After a shooting at Edgewater Technology in Wakefield, Massachusetts, the CEO stated, "Our deepest condolences are with the families of our friends and colleagues who lost their lives in this senseless act of violence. We want all of our employees to know that the company is currently putting in place the necessary counseling and support system."[14] With this statement, the CEO expressed sympathy for victims and reinforced the fact that the organization was also victimized.

The reminder and ingratiation strategies can be used with any crisis. A reminder seeks to call attention to an organization's past good works—after acknowledging the seriousness of the current crisis. Of course, this strategy can be used only when there are past good works. After an explosion at a County Pure facility, the senior vice president of operations stated, "County Pure Foods has always taken very seriously our responsibility to protect human health and safety as well as the environment."[15] This statement reminded people that the company has been a responsible corporate citizen. After a 2003 explosion at a Sigma-Aldrich facility in Miamisburg, Ohio, the CFO said, "We also appreciate and thank our neighbors in Miamisburg who have showed remarkable patience throughout the disruption this has caused in their daily lives."[16] This ingratiation response praises community members affected by the crisis.

As mentioned earlier, modifiers change how people view a crisis. A negative crisis history or unfavorable performance history increases the reputational threat level and thus changes the recommended post-crisis response strategy. Workplace violence and product tampering should be treated as accidental crises, not as victim crises, in companies with one or both modifiers. Technical-error product harm, technical-error accidents, and challenges are considered preventable crises when one or both modifiers are present. Considering modifiers is crucial for matching the post-crisis response strategy to the threat level. The greater the reputational threat, the more the response must be the acknowledgement of responsibility and the addressing of victims' needs.

In summary, here are the SCCT guidelines:

1. For crises with minimal attributions of crisis responsibility (victim crises) in organizations with no history of similar crises and a neutral or positive performance history, instructing and adjusting information can be enough.
2. For workplace violence, product tampering, natural disasters, and rumors, the victimage bolstering strategy can be used.
3. For rumors and challenges, use denial strategies when possible.
4. For crises with minimal attributions of crisis responsibility (victim crises) coupled with a history of similar crises and/or negative performance history, use strategies from the diminishment posture.
5. For crises with low attributions of crisis responsibility (accidental crises) in organizations with no history of similar crises and a neutral or positive performance history, use strategies from the diminishment posture.
6. For crises with low attributions of crisis responsibility (accidental crises), coupled with a history of similar crises and/or negative performance history, use strategies from the rebuilding posture.
7. For crises with strong attributions of crisis responsibility (preventable crises), use strategies from the rebuilding posture regardless of crisis history

and performance history.

8. Use bolstering strategies as supplements to the other strategies.
9. Try to send consistent messages by not mixing denial strategies with either diminishment or rebuilding strategies, both of which acknowledge that there was in fact a crisis.
10. Be prepared to change crisis response strategies if the situation changes.

Constraints to Consider When Using SCCT

In discussing crisis management, we tend to generalize, but we all know that each crisis is unique. Hence, crisis leaders should modify the above recommendations to fit their situations and the constraints of their organizations. One constraint may be financial resources. Can the organization afford the liability assumed with an apology or the costs of changing business practices? If the answer is no, compensation may be a better option that should yield similar reputational benefits. Or the organization could choose the excuse strategy, knowing that it will be less effective but also less costly. An organization faced with challenges to its operating practices might change those practices to avoid negative publicity or deny the charges because it cannot afford the necessary changes.

Organizational culture can also be a constraint. Will management be comfortable responding to a crisis in a way that acknowledges the organization's responsibility and focuses on the victims? For years, Procter & Gamble resisted changing its man-in-the-moon logo—which was rumored to be linked to Satan worship—because the logo had a long history in the company and had become part of its culture. Eventually, however, P&G dropped the logo, which had become a liability.

Finally, a crisis may become a different crisis type. Merck's crisis with Vioxx quickly changed from an accidental crisis, in which the company was unaware of the danger of the drug, to a preventable crisis, in which Merck was accused of having ignored warning signs for more than two years.[17] Merck's post-crisis response shifted from offering instructing information to attacking the validity of the warning signs. Merck's open letter advertisements in the *Wall Street Journal* challenged the earlier evidence that Vioxx was safe.

The SCCT guidelines are not to be followed in lockstep but adjusted to fit the constraints and demands of the particular event. Crisis managers will not always be able to use the post-crisis response strategies that will provide the greatest protection to the organization's reputation. But even the "lesser" strategies will help. The key is for managers to make informed choices about response strategies and to know how and why to adjust those strategies as situations unfold.

1. See W.T. Coombs, "Impact of Past Crises on Current Crisis Communication: Insights from Situational Crisis Communication Theory," *Journal of Business Communication* 41 (2004): 265-289.

2. B. Weiner, "An Attributional Theory of Achievement Motivation and Emotion," *Psychology Review* 92 (1985): 548-573.

3. D.W. Jolly and J.C. Mowen, "Product Recall Communications: The Effects of Source, Media, and Social Responsibility Information," *Advances in Consumer Research* 11 (1984): 471-475.

4. W.T. Coombs and S.J. Holladay, "Communication and Attributions in a Crisis: An Experimental Study of Crisis Communication," *Journal of Public Relations Research* 8 (1996): 279-295.

5. S.J. Ray, *Strategic Communication in Crisis Management: Lessons from the Airline Industry* (Westport, CT: Quorum Books, 1999).

6. P. Herbig, J. Milewicz, and J. Golden, "A Model of Reputation Building and Destruction," *Journal of Business Research* 31(1994): 23-31.

7. W.T. Coombs and S.J. Holladay, "Helping Crisis Managers Protect Reputational Assets: Initial Tests of the Situational Crisis Communication Theory," *Management Communication Quarterly* 16 (2002): 165-186

8. R. Ahluwalia, R.E. Burnkrant, and H.R. Unnava, "Consumer Response to Negative Publicity: The Moderating Role of Commitment," *Journal of Marketing Research* 27 (2000): 203-214; N. Dawar and M.M. Pillutla, "Impact of Product-harm Crises on Brand Equity: The Moderating Role of Consumer Expectations," *Journal of Marketing Research* 27 (2000): 215-226; D.H. Dean, "Consumer Reaction to Negative Publicity: Effects of Corporate Reputation, Response, and Responsibility for a Crisis Event," *Journal of Business Communication* 41 (2004): 192-211.

9. M.W. Allen and R.H. Caillouet, "Legitimate Endeavors: Impressionmanagement Strategies Used by an Organization in Crisis," *Communication Monographs* 61 (1994): 44-62; W.L. Benoit, *Accounts, Excuses, and Apologies: A Theory of Image Restoration* (Albany, NY: State University of New York Press, 1995).

10. K. Potts, "Advertisers Not 'Desperate,'" 20 Oct. 2004, eonline, 9 Dec. 2004. http://www.eonline.com/News?Items/Pf/0,1527,15181,00.html; "Fast-Food Restaurant Agrees to Improve Animal Welfare Standards," 6 Sept. 2001, PETA, 9 Dec. 2004. http://peta.org/news/NewsItem.asp?id=360.

11. V. Johnson and S. Peppas, "Crisis Management in Belgium: The Case of Coca-Cola," *Corporate Communications: An International Journal* 8 (2003): 18-22; A. Milligan,

"Preparedness Can Temper Effects of Product Recall," Business Insurance 33 (15 March 1999): 6.

12. E. Denzenhall, *Nail 'em: Confronting High Profile Attacks on Celebrities & Businesses* (Amherst, NY: Prometheus Books, 2003).

13. A. Patel and L. Reinsch, "Companies Can Apologize: Corporate Apologies and Legal Liability," *Business Communication Quarterly* 66 (2003): 17-26; L. Tyler, "Liability Means Never Being Able to Say You're Sorry: Corporate Guilt, Legal Constraints, and Defensiveness in Corporate Communication," *Management Communication Quarterly* 11(1997): 51-73.

14. "Statement by Edgewater Technology," 26 Dec. 2000, Edgewater Technology, 12 Jan. 2001. http://www.edgewater.com/site/news_events/press_releases/122700_wakefield.html.

15. "Statement from Paul Sukalich, Senior Vice President of Operations," 14 Oct. 2003, Country Pure Foods, 14 Oct. 2003. http://www.purecountry.com/inthenews_pressreleases.html.

16. "Sigma-Aldrich plant damaged by explosion," 22 Sept. 2003, Sigma-Aldrich, 29 Sept. 2003. http://www.corporate-ir.net/ireye.

17. "FDA failed public on Vioxx, official says," 18 Nov. 2004, MSNBC, 8 Nov. 2004. http://msnbc.msn.com/id/6520630/print/1/displaymode/1098/.

On the CD-ROM

1. See *Biggest Challenges Organizations Face Today,* Christophe Roux-Dufort, "Legitimacy and Reputation."

2. See *Learning to Be a Crisis Leader,* Kathleen Sutcliffe, "Seek Feedback."

3. See *Biggest Challenges Organizations Face Today,* Bill McCloskey, "Ignoring the Little Things."

4. See *Biggest Challenges Organizations Face Today,* Bill McCloskey, "Identifying Problems."

5. See *Biggest Challenges Organizations Face Today,* David Shapiro, "Corporate Reputation."

6. See *Learning to Be a Crisis Leader,* Kathleen Sutcliffe, "Set the Tone."

CHAPTER 5

Using Apologies to Overcome the Bumps in the Road to Redemption

David B. Wooten is an assistant professor of marketing at the University of Michigan's Ross School of Business, where he also earned his M.B.A. and Ph.D. His research focuses on impression management by individual and organizational actors. Wooten's current projects examine the use of apologies in crisis communication. His writings have appeared in book chapters and academic journals such as the Journal of Consumer Research, *the* Journal of Consumer Psychology, *and* Advances in Consumer Research.

by David B. Wooten

IT USED TO BE THAT AN organizational apology was a rare event. Leaders once eschewed them as a sign of weakness, and legal staffs saw them as a form of self-incrimination[1] —"Anything you say can and will be used against you in a court of law." But consider these recent examples of high-profile apologies for various transgressions:

- In 2000, the chairman of United Airlines was featured in a television commercial apologizing to travelers who endured flight cancellations and poor customer service during a labor dispute.

- In 2001, officials from Ford and Firestone issued a videotaped apology to expedite a settlement with a woman who was paralyzed in an accident involving a Ford Explorer equipped with defective Firestone tires. The woman reportedly settled her lawsuit for a third of the $100 million she originally sought.[2]
- In 2002, the chairman of Boston Beer Co. apologized in newspaper ads following public outrage and boycott threats over his appearance on a radio show that ran a "Sex for Sam" contest, in which couples competed for prizes by having sex in public places. The radio show aired a live broadcast of a couple allegedly having sex in New York's St. Patrick's Cathedral.
- In 2003, the management team for the Los Angeles-based Pat & Oscar's restaurant chain ran a newspaper ad in the *San Diego Union-Tribune* apologizing for having served tainted lettuce, which resulted in eight confirmed, 45 probable, and two suspected E. coli infections.
- In 2004, Keysor-Century Corp., a California-based plastics manufacturer, was forced to take out a full-page newspaper ad to apologize for spewing carcinogenic chemicals into the air and pumping potent toxins into a nearby river. The apology was part of a settlement agreement that also included a $4.3 million penalty.

Why the proliferation of apologies? Crisis management and public relations experts attribute it to the lessons learned from Johnson & Johnson's effective response to the Tylenol crisis and President Clinton's ineffective response to the infamous Lewinski affair.[3] Johnson & Johnson salvaged its reputation when leaders immediately took responsibility for a crisis caused by events that many people believed were beyond the company's control, whereas President Clinton tarnished his reputation when he failed to accept responsibility for creating a problem for which many people held him accountable. The pharmaceutical giant was applauded for thinking first of its customer relationships, and the former president was criticized for thinking only of himself. This contrast of responses and outcomes highlights the benefits of treating reputations and relationships as strategic assets. The potential for apologies to help salvage relationships and restore reputations has undoubtedly contributed to their recent proliferation.

This chapter summarizes the theories and evidence of how apologies address these two bumps in the road to redemption, considers characteristics of apologies and their effects, and presents a framework to suggest when apologies should be offered.

How Apologies Heal Damaged Relationships

Authors of an early compilation of research on equity theory identified various means by which apologies enable transgressors to restore balance to damaged relationships.[4] According to equity theory, individuals perceive disparities and feel distressed when they are adversely affected by the transgressions of others. Consequently, they adjust what they think, feel, or do about transgressors to reduce inequities in their relationships and minimize the pain of feeling cheated. In order to preempt victims' efforts to reevaluate their relationships and perhaps to seek justice or revenge, transgressors can take the initiative to restore equity by apologizing to victims.

Apologies require transgressors to humble themselves and exalt their victims. The redistribution of esteem rewards victims and punishes transgressors, thereby offsetting some of the harm to the relationships. A prominent psychologist expressed similar sentiments about the healing power of apologies when he asserted, "What makes apologies work is an exchange of shame and power between offender and offended. By apologizing, you take the shame of your offense and redirect it to yourself. You admit to hurting or diminishing someone and, in effect, say that you are really the one who is diminished …In acknowledging your shame, you give the offended the power to forgive. The exchange is at the heart of the healing process."[5] He also stated that successful apologies convey suffering and soul-searching regret. Such expressions enable apologizers to restore equity by prompting victims to reevaluate the magnitude of the inequities in their relationships with transgressors.

Research in services marketing supports the notion that apologies influence perceptions of fairness. For instance, apologies have been found to shape customers' beliefs about how fairly they have been treated, which, in turn, affects their satisfaction with the service they have received, their intentions to do business with the company in the future, and whether they will share their positive or negative experiences with others. At a VA hospital in Lexington, Kentucky, for instance, officials reported a substantial decline in malpractice payments and litigation costs after implementing a policy of taking responsibility for mistakes, disclosing them to patients, and apologizing for them.

How Apologies Restore Tarnished Reputations

Impression-management theory sheds light on the use of apologies to safeguard or restore reputations. Proponents of this perspective argue that social actors use apologies to influence what people infer about them as a result of their transgressions, thereby influencing how others expect them to behave in future interactions. "Apologies are designed to convince the audience that the undesirable event should not be considered a fair representation of what the actor is 'really like.'"[6] The apologizer does this by blaming a "self" that no longer exists or has changed sufficiently to reduce concerns about repeat offenses. In essence, the apologizer "splits himself into two parts, the part that is guilty of an offense and the part that dissociates itself from the delict and affirms a belief in the offended rule."[7] The apologizer attempts to enable the "good" self to move forward while leaving the "bad" self behind, discredited and vilified.

Complete apologies convey regret, acknowledge expected behavior and the costs of misbehavior, repudiate bad behavior and the self that misbehaved, espouse proper behavior and promise it in the future, and show penance and offer restitution.[8] Collectively, these elements reflect an effort to undo the past and restore faith. Expressing regret and offering restitution suggest the actor has paid an emotional penalty and is willing to make amends. Acknowledging the rules, castigating the self for violating them, and promising future adherence to rules suggest the actor knows better and intends to behave better. In other words, complete apologies suggest that severe penalties are unnecessary and future problems are unlikely.

Research in psychology highlights the potential for apologies to offset damage to reputations. Various studies have shown that individuals who apologize for their transgressions are evaluated more favorably than those who do not. Apologetic transgressors are especially likely to be held in higher regard than their unapologetic counterparts when their apologies are not merely perfunctory, they are not suspected of having dubious motives, and they already have good reputations. Apologetic transgressors are more likely than unapologetic ones to be described in such favorable terms as responsible, sincere, and careful. The type of transgression influences how effectively apologies restore reputations. Apologizers have been found to recover more easily from mistakes that raise questions about their abilities than from misdeeds that raise questions about their integrity. Evidently, people find it easier to believe that smart people can make dumb mistakes than to accept that good people can do bad things.

The Art of Crafting Apologies

Recent articles in the business and popular press have included expert advice on crafting and issuing organizational apologies. These discussions often focus on three aspects of apologies: content, source, and timing. These important aspects and their effects on relationships and reputations are considered below.

Content. The question of whether or not to admit responsibility for harm has been debated in discussions of the appropriate content of apologies. The argument against admitting responsibility is often based on legal advice to avoid self-incrimination, thereby minimizing the probability of being found guilty in the event of a lawsuit. The primary concern is to avoid providing ammunition to alleged victims who are likely to retaliate by pursuing litigation. The argument in favor of acknowledging fault is based on a belief that an admission of responsibility is a clear signal of a commitment to repair damage to relationships or reputations. The gist of the argument is that those who fess up can redeem themselves by putting their relationships ahead of their pride and blaming a self that is eager to improve. These efforts are expected to result in lower probabilities of retaliation by alleged victims and smaller penalties sought by or awarded to those who retaliate. Toro, the manufacturer of lawn mowers, may have designed a mediation process that offers the rewards of apologies without the risk of self-incrimination. The process begins with an expression of deep regret to injured customers but does not include an admission of fault. As a result of this process, Toro has not defended itself in court since 1994, and 95 percent of the company's cases are settled on the day of mediation or shortly thereafter.[9]

Source. Expert opinion on who should issue apologies typically converges on organizational leaders as ideal sources. The belief that apologies must come from the top reflects the sentiment that a contrite leader is a powerful signal that the organization values the relationships that were damaged and plans to make the changes necessary to do better in the future. The need for such powerful signals may increase with the magnitude of harm and the number of victims. However, apologies from the actual culprits or their immediate supervisors should be sufficient for minor problems with few victims.

Timing. Two clichés sum up popular wisdom on the optimal timing of apologies: "The sooner the better," but "Better late than never." Lengthy intervals between transgressions and apologies raise questions about the extent to which apologizers value the relationships they damaged or espouse the rules they violated. Delayed apologies may be less likely than timely ones to facilitate reconciliation, but they still can diminish hostility from victims. Moreover, delayed apologies may be less effective at restoring tarnished reputations because they raise doubts about the character and sincerity of the apologizers, and they prolong a focus on the transgressions and the type of actors who commit them.

Owing Apologies

As admissions of blameworthiness, apologies suggest that a guilty verdict is warranted. However, as expressions of remorse, they suggest that the actor does not have the character flaws that are commonly associated with people who commit similar transgressions. In other words, apologizers are likely to escape some, but not all, negative repercussions associated with a guilty verdict. For this reason, people may be most likely to apologize for their transgressions when the probability of being blamed is high or the cost of accepting blame is low.[10] The preceding analysis highlights conditions when organizations feel safe apologizing, but it does not consider when their audiences feel entitled to apologies.

People's expectations of receiving apologies depend, in part, on their beliefs about the causes and effects of the problems they encounter. According to the framework presented below, people feel entitled to apologies for problems caused by intentional misdeeds or problems with adverse effects that could have been foreseen and prevented. These problems suggest malice and negligence, respectively. People should feel less entitled to apologies when they are victims of problems with uncontrollable causes and unpreventable effects, problems with uncontrollable causes and unforeseeable effects, or problems with unintentional causes and unforeseeable effects.

Conditions When Apologies Are Expected

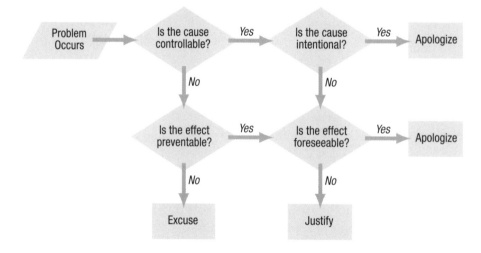

Conclusion

In the past, apologies were discouraged out of fear that they would facilitate litigation, thereby making bad situations worse for organizations in crises. The focus on avoiding worst case scenarios may have prevented organizations from pursuing more favorable outcomes. In the case of apologies, the rewards may outweigh the risks: in addition to their effects on constituents whose relationships were harmed during crises, apologies have reputational effects that extend to constituents who were not directly affected. It is quite conceivable that these unaffected onlookers constitute the primary audience for a growing number of highly publicized apologies that we observe today.

---

1. K. Frieswick, "Say You're Sorry: In Some Lawsuits, Falling on Your Sword May Be Smarter Than Wielding It," *CFO.Com: Tools and Resources for Financial Executives,* May 1, 2001, www.cfo.com/Article?article=2922.

2. P.J. Kiger, "The Art of the Apology," *Workforce Management* 83 (10) (2004): 57-62.

3. J. Frank, "Sorry Is No Longer the Hardest Word," *Marketing Focus,* 2000, http://www.marketing.haynet.com/feature00/1012/.

4. E. Walster, G.W. Walster, and E. Berscheid, *Equity: Theory and Research* (Boston: Allyn and Bacon, 1978).

5. A. Lazare, "Go Ahead Say You're Sorry," *Psychology Today* 28(January/February 1995): 40-43, 76, 78.

6. B.R. Schlenker, *Impression Management: The Self-Concept, Social Identity, and Interpersonal Relations* (Montery, CA: Brooks/Cole Publishing, 1980).

7. E. Goffman, *Relations in Public* (New York: Basic Books, 1971).

8. Ibid.

9. V. Liberman, "Why Not Say You're Sorry?" *Across the Board* 41(6)(2004): 36.

10. Schlenker, *Impression Management.*

On the CD-ROM

 See *Learning to Be a Crisis Leader,* Bill McCloskey, "Training."

CHAPTER 6

Putting Panic in Perspective

by Mary J. Waller

Mary J. Waller is an associate professor of organizational behavior at Tulane University's A.B. Freeman School of Business. Her research focuses on team dynamics under crisis and time-pressured situations, and includes studies of commercial airline flight crews, nuclear power plant crews, and emergency medical response teams. Waller earned her Ph.D. from the University of Texas at Austin.

PANIC IS NOT A SUBJECT typically discussed in M.B.A. classrooms or by the business press. We want to believe (and organizations certainly want stockholders to believe) that our problem-solving models and processes, even during times of stress and crisis, lead to rational, well-grounded decisions. In fact, if you delve deeply into what has been written on management over the past 50 years or so, you will find few mentions of the "p" word.

Yet we know that panic is a hardwired, largely unavoidable human response to threat. And it exists for a good reason. When our ancestors came face-to-face with a mortal threat, they experienced a rush of adrenaline that focused their senses, made their hearts pound, and increased the likelihood of their success in either fight or flight. In psychological terms, they experienced attentional narrowing, which focused everything they had on the situation at hand.

And that type of focused response—both psychological and physiological—worked pretty well for the threats of the day. The problem today is that our ingrained panic response does not work so well with the types of threats we now face. Unlike the menacing saber-toothed tiger, our threats emanate from complex and dynamic events. A tiger remains a tiger—fast, lethal, armed with teeth and claws. But an unexpected product defect can quickly morph into a variety of simultaneous threats, such as class action suits, plummeting stock prices, cancelled mergers, an outraged public, or worse. The attentional narrowing of a panic response can lead us to shut out vital information about an emergent, changing, threatening situation. We end up operating with tunnel vision, immediately latching on to a definition of the situation and course of action, without stopping to update either in the face of new information.

A panic-induced response to a threat can also initiate rash behavior. When confronted with his or her own error or slip of ethical judgment, how many managers immediately deny responsibility, only to admit later that they panicked under attack? How many hastily sent e-mails, written as a knee-jerk, panic-motivated reaction to a negative surprise or threat, have permanently damaged relationships inside and outside organizations? Conversely, we all can think of colleagues or competitors who have displayed the panic-induced alternative to such damaging behavior: the stunned, seemingly frozen, "deer in the headlights" response to a crisis situation.

Although the crises and threats we face in organizations are usually not life threatening, they can be hugely consequential to our careers and organizations. And even if extinguishing all panic in the face of threat is impossible, managers may be able to minimize such responses if they know something about the characteristics of individuals, groups, and organizations that increase the probability of panic-induced decisions and responses. But why is this knowledge suddenly useful today, particularly given that the management literature has basically ignored the issue of panic for years? As it turns out, examining the role of panic in organizations earlier was simply not that relevant for the majority of organizations, scholars, or managers. This is not to suggest that panic in organizations did not occur, but the likelihood of its occurrence and the magnitude of its consequences were fairly contained. But times have certainly changed. Today, there are three key factors that make situations especially ripe for panic-induced behaviors in organizations. First, though, just what exactly is panic?

A Panic Primer

Is panic an emotion or a behavior? The question has been batted around by sociologists and psychologists for years. Based on reports from those who have survived crises, being in a state of panic can lead to a variety of behaviors (fight, flight, total inaction); thus, it is difficult to label panic as one behavior. It may be more useful to think of panic as a state of being that follows fear. The word *panic* comes from Pan, the Greek god who loved to frighten away unsuspecting travelers. According to the *Oxford English Dictionary,* panic involves "exhibiting unreasoning, groundless, or excessive fear" resulting from a real or imagined threat. Panic-inducing fear goes beyond an everyday, mild stress-inducing fear—for example, the fear of being late to a meeting. At the far end of the spectrum, and beyond our focus here, is the panic-induced behavior that individuals exhibit in the face of physical danger. Also beyond our focus are panic attacks and other panic-related pathological disorders. Rather than being caused by mortal danger or psychological issues, the panic-inducing fears experienced by organizational decision makers result from unexpected, complex, and unmistakably consequential events—those involving careers, key clients, large sums of money, public reputation, legal action, and the like. The fear generated by such events can lead decision makers to experience two key needs—needs they are compelled to satisfy—that affect their subsequent actions.

The first is the pressing need to escape the situation. Decision makers acting to satisfy this need may make irrational or rash decisions simply to get out of a threatening situation quickly, much like the flight response of those in physical danger. For example, individual investors often panic and hastily sell off positions in the face of unexpected threatening economic or market news. Similarly, the unexpected threat of legal action may lead decision makers inexperienced with such threats to agree to a settlement without determining if a settlement is in the best interests of the firm. Other escape maneuvers include denying the situation's severity, blaming others, and freezing or ignoring the situation entirely—decidedly not the behaviors associated with effective decision making in today's organizations.

Flight-oriented escape behavior may be what most of us envision when we think of panic, but there is a second need that probably motivates more panicked behavior among managers in organizations: the need to regain control. Although we like to think we can roll with the punches, being in a crisis situation imbued with ambiguity and surprises at every turn can make even the most seasoned manager feel like a nerve-jangled character in a Hitchcock film. Most managers are highly motivated to regain control over such situations, not only to reduce fear of the unknown but also to protect their reputations in organizations that place a high value on being in control. Decision makers used to being on top of every situation may feel panicked when confronted by an unexpected, threatening event and may respond by becoming irrationally rigid, inflexible, and control-bound in a still-developing situation. The need for control is more likely to create a fight response than a flight response. And fighting for control in a crisis situation is what managers are supposed to do, right? Yes, to a certain extent, but they are also supposed to be continually updating information and adapting to changes in the situation. Unfortunately, the rigidity of the panic-induced approach to controlling crises can harm entire organizations. Recently, for example, the makers of Kryptonite bicycle locks were taken by surprise when a spate of Internet postings claimed that the locks could easily be opened with a ballpoint pen. The company rebuffed the claim, offering routine assurances regarding the locks' steel strength and integrity, which effectively gave Internet bloggers the opportunity and time to post a video demonstrating the pen technique to their mushrooming audience. The cost to Kryptonite after only seven days of rigid response? Approximately $10 million (the cost of giving replacement locks to a now enormous public alerted both by bloggers and by numerous articles about the firm's delayed response).[1] A panic-induced, rigid response to a crisis is somewhat insidious in that it may make us feel like we're controlling the situation, but it is unlikely to give us the results we want.

Interestingly, both escape- and control-oriented behaviors often follow a well-learned course of action—a logical path that has been practiced enough to become an ingrained habit.[2] Under extreme pressure, we engage in practiced behaviors. For example, individuals trapped in a burning building will often run not to the closest exit but to the one they use most frequently. Similarly, have you ever experienced a computer glitch during an important presentation and responded by rapidly typing well-learned commands over and over, hoping for a magical result that puts you back in control? Can you hear your heart pounding and feel your mouth go dry as people shift uncomfortably in their seats? Unfortunately, these physiological manifestations of panic, along with the reduced information processing that accompanies attentional narrowing, severely limit a decision maker's ability to think outside the box, which is exactly the kind of thinking most needed at such moments. Although the examples of panic-induced behavior above might lead us to the impression that panic is a "people" problem—so let's solve it by hiring people who don't do that—the issue of panic in today's organizations stretches well beyond the individual. We are all prone to feeling panicked in certain situations; unfortunately, the likelihood that decision makers in organizations will wind up embroiled in true panic-inducing situations has significantly increased, as has the magnitude of consequences stemming from panic-induced behavior. Three central factors are to blame.

Ripe for Panic

Most organization scholars agree that business environments have become more complex, unpredictable, and turbulent over the past two decades.[3] The new environment, because of its increased complexity, serves up unexpected crises with which managers have little experience. What has changed that increases the variety of unexpected threats? First, in addition to the Internet-stoked pace of much business today, new competitors are emerging overnight. Agreements that heretofore would have created the most unlikely alliances (Chrysler and Daimler-Benz, for instance) are now rapidly producing new competition with wide-reaching effects. Likewise, technology such as genetic engineering is making once-barren fields fertile and once-marginalized producers powerful competitors (such as Brazilian soybean producers). The advent of online business-to-business contract bidding and Internet-based trading is leveling the playing field and increasing competition in formerly staid markets. The cumulative result of these and many more new sources of competition is that decision makers must monitor more information, consider more actions, and anticipate new, unfamiliar types of crises precipitated by often unknown competitors who do not necessarily behave like yesterday's rivals. And unexpected, potentially lethal attacks by unfamiliar competitors—attacks that must be countered under time pressure—create situations ripe for classic panic-motivated responses.

Second, many organizations are dealing with the increased variety and velocity of threats and crises by decentralizing decision making and creating decision-making teams. On the surface, this makes sense. Decentralization pushes decision-making authority down to the individuals and teams on the front lines, who then don't have to waste time waiting for approval from the top. Likewise, using teams to make key decisions brings a wider variety of perspectives to bear on the crisis at hand. However, while decentralization increases the speed of decision making, it also gives authority to those least able to draw on previous experiences when facing an unexpected, unfamiliar crisis. Combined with the competitive environment described above, some decentralization schemes may ultimately match the most inexperienced managers with the most complex crises, thus setting up wildly unfamiliar situations likely to induce panicked responses. Similarly, firms with offices in several locations that want to leverage team decision making must deploy geographically distributed teams; however, teams whose members are in different locations are often unable to leverage the rich nonverbal communication and other resources that co-located teams depend on in fast decision-making situations, and they may find it virtually impossible to achieve a shared understanding of an unfolding crisis.[4] Stir in cultural differences, and the result can be a quagmire of miscommunication and mistrust, leading to an uncertain, stressful, chaotic, and contagious panic-induced response.

Finally, communication technology can both inflame panic and create its own panic-inducing fear. As we know from studies of bank runs and crowd behavior, panic is contagious. This is also true inside organizations, where panic can be spread through e-mail systems and Web sites. Consider what happened at a successful customer relationship management (CRM) software company when employees learned of management's top-secret layoff plans by going to the online HR database and checking their paid time-off balances—any employee whose balance was zeroed out was getting the axe.[5] Panic spread like wildfire via e-mail through offices around the world, with some employees walking out and others yelling at bewildered local managers. The situation forced management to scuttle its plans, and the CEO sent an e-mail apology to all concerned. In other instances, a single wrong keystroke has created a panic-prone situation by broadcasting an error. For example, an analyst at Lehman Brothers mistakenly sent a confidential e-mail about a colleague's plans to leave the firm to 75 clients instead of to another colleague.[6] Realizing his mistake, the analyst immediately sent a second e-mail asking the clients not to read the first message—a control-motivated action that, in hindsight, made the first message more irresistible reading that it ever could have been originally.

Our inability to hit the "undo" button once electronic information is transmitted or posted can help us create our very own panic-inducing crises. Consider the fate of the president of the Association for Local Telecommunication Services, after his highly sensitive strategic lobbying plan was mistakenly e-mailed to the Federal Communications Commission (FCC) along with other documents as part of an electronic filing procedure. Although the plan was posted on the FCC's Web site for only three hours before the mistake was recognized, it was long enough for lobbyists, lawyers, and industry insiders to download it, and for journalists to print excerpts from it. According to the *Washington Post,* "(t)he disclosure of the candid document embarrassed ALTS and subjected it to ridicule among other lobbying organizations."[7] More important for the organization, "There was a danger that the publication of the document could jeopardize ALTS's credibility with several of the key (FCC) policymakers."[8] The president promptly resigned after the incident.

Conclusion

Many of the survival instincts we inherited from our ancestors—including panic—serve us quite well. We want a panic response to supercharge our physical reaction to mortal threat. Notwithstanding the unfortunate reality of terrorism and workplace violence, though, physical danger in our daily environments has been replaced by M&A negotiations, class action suits, scandals, and mistakes. But our panic response is alive and well, and is playing havoc with our ability to deal successfully with today's crises.

What to do? Increasing the ability of managers to recognize panic-induced behavior may go a long way in helping them replace such behavior with more measured and informed responses to critical events. Of course, increasing this ability and awareness is not without hurdles. First, many of us have come to believe that in business environments running at Internet speed, fast equals good. Depending on the crisis, a fast response may indeed be imperative, but this axiom also creates an expectation for fast response in virtually every crisis, in effect giving people carte blanche to panic. It could be that the extra measure of speed is costing far more than it is worth, and that a slightly slower but more informed response would be more effective. But developing knowledge about when to touch the brakes requires taking a retrospective look at an organization's threats and crises, and helping managers classify them into rough categories based on the speed with which they must be handled. Many firms are simply not able or willing to invest the time necessary for this kind of analysis, but the payoffs of such an exercise over time could be significant. Second, loosening the death grip of control during an unfolding crisis cuts against the grain of many managers who are rewarded on the basis of their ability to control and coordinate. Reprogramming our ingrained panic-induced responses to threat may require simulator training programs similar to those developed for pilots and nuclear power plant operators.

The "p" word in and of itself may carry some stigma in management settings, which makes it difficult to have open conversations with managers about past panic-induced behavior and how to avoid it. Many of us are motivated to use a bit of revisionist history when it comes to panic: if we panicked and chanced into a good outcome, we tend to relabel our behavior as "decisive." Getting managers to admit and discuss past panicked behavior may take some prodding. But with practice, managers can learn how to deal with panic in organizations. Awareness is the crucial first step.

1. D. Kirkpatrick and D. Roth, "Why There's No Escaping the Blog," *Fortune,* December 27, 2004.

2. B.M. Staw, L.E. Sandelands, and J.E. Dutton, "Threat Rigidity Effects in Organizational Behavior: A Multilevel Analysis," *Administrative Science Quarterly* 26 (1981): 501-524.

3. M.J. Waller and K.H. Roberts, "High Reliability and Organizational Behavior: Finally the Twain Must Meet," *Journal of Organizational Behavior* 24 (2003): 813-814.

4. M.L. Maznevski and K.M. Chudoba, "Bridging Space Over Time: Global Virtual Team Dynamics and Effectiveness," *Organization Science* 11 (2000): 473-492.

5. L.A. Perlow and D.L. Ager, "The Cat Is Out of the Bag: KANA and the Layoff Gone Awry," Boston, MA: Harvard Business School Publishing, 2003.

6. R.T. King, "Misdirected E-mail Offers a Glimpse into Office Politics—Lehman Analyst Sends File to Colleague, but Clients Get the Message Too" *Wall Street Journal* (Eastern edition), New York, NY, December 4, 1998, p. 1

7. J.H. Birnbaum and C. Stern, "Phone Group Head Resigns After Uproar," *Washington Post,* October 6, 2004, section E, p. 1.

8. Ibid.

On the CD-ROM

(1) See *Biggest Challenges Organizations Face Today,* Christophe Roux-Dufort, "Risk Management."

(2) See *Learning to Be a Crisis Leader,* David Shapiro, "Allow Disconfirming Data to Be Heard."

(3) See *Learning to Be a Crisis Leader,* Bill McCloskey, "Who Is Responsible?"

CHAPTER 7

Managing and Avoiding Outrage

by Garth Rowan

Garth Rowan has two decades of experience as a communications strategist, broadcast reporter, and lawyer. He specializes in outrage management, stakeholder relations, crisis communication, mediation, and interest based negotiation. His work takes him to breakdowns in communication in North and South America and Europe.

C ONTROVERSIAL PLANT SITINGS, spills, explosions, injuries, deaths: these are just some of the flashpoints today for confrontation between David and Goliath. Outraged communities at loggerheads with powerful institutions abound. Organizations, whether they are big corporations or big government, are increasingly frustrated at not getting what whey want and are rarely clear about the reasons. The result is a contentious, litigious, and distrustful society. We need communities and corporations to get on better. That's not to suggest they should be buddies—that would be false and short-lived, not to mention impossible within the capitalist structure—but for the sake of society we have to do better.

My goal here is to explain the tensions between communities and corporations and explore ways of resolving them. I have applied to my observations and experiences from the field the rich insights of Vince Covello of the Center for Risk Communication, Peter

Sandman of the Center for Environmental Communication at Rutgers University, and Lawrence Susskind and Patrick Field from MIT. These pioneers have led the way in the study of effective communication of risk and ways to manage and avoid public outrage. The goal of such work is to reduce tensions and improve the dialogue between organizations and stakeholders, which will lead to better decisions for all.

Locked into Position

Clearly there are faults on both sides, but my focus is on the corporate sector because it possesses more of the structures and internal cohesion to take on the role of the proactive party. Historically, corporations have almost en masse missed the causes of outrage among stakeholders. Take the example of the company that planned to build a potentially high-risk operation a few hundred yards away from a family's home. The company introduced the plan to the family by delivering a leaflet containing instructions on how to evacuate in the event of a poison gas release. The outraged family worked up a coalition that defeated the project while subjecting the company to national ridicule. Or consider the company that wanted to expand in the community in which it had been operating for 30 years. The company, which had never developed a community relations program, was shocked by the reaction of community members, who had been waiting 30 years for payback for past slights, real or perceived, and mired the company in acrimonious, costly, and time-consuming hearings.

Few protagonists are totally right or totally wrong. For their part, corporations complain that there is too much legislation; they argue that increased traffic, polluted air, noise, and ruined vistas are the price of economic development, the price of living in an industrialized society from which we all benefit, directly and indirectly. Many of the complainers, they argue, are the end users of the production they are complaining about. Anyway, some corporations say, we only have to pretend to listen. Put a butterfly on the cover of the annual report and use recycled paper. Hold an open house for the complainers—but make sure activists don't hijack the event.

On the other side, stakeholders find themselves struggling to find evidence to back up organizations' claims that "We put people first." Distrustful and outraged community members say no to almost everything corporations suggest and insist that the only acceptable level of risk for their community is zero. When community members fear that a company's plans may pose a risk, their strategy is often to exaggerate the danger and phone the media—actions that only heighten the hostility on both sides.

The problem is that each side is entrenched in its own position and focused on one-sided solutions. Neither side truly understands the issues and interests that drive the other's position. This positional—and oppositional—structure has turned into a battleground.

Look behind a successful corporation quietly getting along with stakeholders and you will find it has a heightened understanding of their concerns, hopes, expectations, assumptions, priorities, beliefs, values, fears, and needs. For example, faced with a community that opposes the building of a new plant, a company can either immediately storm onto the battlefield or explore the interests behind the community's position. One vivid example of the latter approach was a company that discovered that the future of a soccer club was the main concern for a community opposed to a company's proposed plant. As one community member explained, "My kids play soccer on that land you want to put your plant on, and their team will have to be disbanded. The team is my main source of social interaction, and my best friends are other parents—you are jeopardizing my important relationships." The issue for this individual was not actually the plant site but the future of the soccer club. Equipped with this understanding of the community's concerns, the company was able to pursue a more productive approach. Imagine how futile it was for the engineering staff to argue about the merits of the plant site with families connected to the soccer club! It turned out to be fairly easy to find a new venue for the soccer club, and in the end, the new plant, the soccer club, and social relationships were able to thrive in the same community.

The need for listening and probing for interests goes both ways. Communities must reciprocate by developing an understanding of what drives the organizations with which they are at odds. They need to ask what about a certain project keeps their corporate opponents awake at night: jobs, mortgage payments, family stability, bosses, their children's education? The main obstacle to listening is the loudness of the outrage, which in turn tends to alienate the other side and exacerbate the situation. Yet outraged stakeholders have learned that an effective way to get on the corporate radar screen is to make a lot of noise. Remember, they are outraged because they believe their position is being ignored. They realize, of course, that if the majority of people shared their outrage the corporation would have no choice but to deal with the issue. But in reality, noisemakers are few in number at the start of campaigns. This is not truly a problem; as with most things in life, it's the most passionate and committed participants who drive change. As Margaret Mead's ubiquitous motivational quote states: "Never doubt that a small group of thoughtful, committed citizens can change the world. Indeed, it is the only thing that ever has."

Peter Sandman's research shows that a common failing among corporations is their tendency to focus less on the noisemakers and more on winning over the silent majority. Public relations theory tells corporations that this is the most important audience because it is the largest. But that confuses PR with stakeholder relations; the latter requires that relevant detail be given to those affected. The majority is silent for good reason; they are neither informed nor do they care about the issue, perhaps because they are not sufficiently touched by it.

Who are the noisemakers? The loudest are the people most actively opposed to a project. They may be those with the most to lose if something goes wrong—unwilling victims driven by self-interest or even self-preservation. Or they may be professional activists who are opposed on ideological grounds and are therefore forbidden on moral grounds from contributing to a solution. Their goal is to expose the issue and then move on, thus avoiding the stigma of working with "the corporate beast." It is possible to negotiate with all kinds of noisemakers, discover their interests, and collaborate with them to reach a solution. Some strategies include power sharing for those pursuing solutions, the formation of action groups, or arranging for concessions, publicity, recognition, or consulting work.

The Courage to Lose Face

Why are listening and understanding so hard? Why don't corporations see the potential for outrage and defuse it before the community's opposition congeals? Typical responses tend to be, "What does that mean exactly?" "It's not part of my job!" " I don't have time." In examining this problem, Sandman came up with this brilliant equation: Risk = Hazard + Outrage. If I may attempt to reframe this, it might also be expressed as Consent = Respect + Skill. In other words, corporations are given a license to operate (Consent) only when they demonstrate that they have heard and understood the other side (Respect) and that they or their employees have demonstrated a track record of operating their business safely (Skill). The order is important here; as Covello emphasizes, people don't care what you know until they know that you care.

Seems simple enough! Let's look at what corporate leaders can do to meet the terms of the equation.

Respect tends to be at the heart of the battle; the lack of it breeds the cynicism that is rampant on both sides. It starts at the top: Leaders can begin by fostering a culture of respect both inside their companies as well as in the communities in which they operate. They need to admit that they don't know it all, that they can learn from non-technical people, that their agendas and value systems are not the only valid ones, that there are interests beyond financial ones, and that they are not infallible.

That can be a tough sell. It's difficult for a big ego, backed by a lot of success, to confess to not having all the answers. Indeed, many senior executives would rather lose money than lose face. That might explain why there are so many poor decisions out there and why it takes companies and their leaders so long to get their stakeholder relations right.

The kind of ego-driven behavior that we see in so many leaders speaks to an innate desire (or is it a need?) to look good publicly at all times. Overcoming that behavior is about having the courage to lose face. It's also about the bottom-line value of what's good for business in the long term. Avoiding a crisis is cheaper than fixing one. I worked with a CEO whose company wanted to double its oil production in a community. The problem was that the company had got off on the wrong foot with this community by making firm promises and then breaking them. The CEO was dismayed by what his team had done, but, as he saw it, although the company had no "social license," it did have a legal license to operate. His impulse was to resort to the courts and hammer the project through. However, he knew that this project was crucial for the company's future, and he foresaw that a long-term acrimonious relationship with the community would be like living with the flu for life. Eventually, he agreed to attend the next meeting and address the community. He was greeted by a hostile mood that mellowed when he expressed his embarrassment for the broken promises and offered a sincere personal apology. He shocked some hardliners when he asked the community for forgiveness. He also offered a plan to make sure the same thing wouldn't happen again and gave his personal contact information in case people felt that the company was not living up to the new relationship. The community applauded him for his courage in facing them and grudgingly gave his company another chance. Occasional inquiries do come through to his office and are dealt with immediately. As a result, the community and company are moving forward together.

While this CEO unquestionably gained respect in the eyes of the community, some may say he lost face in his world. His enemies could crow of how he was brought to his knees by a bunch of rednecks. That can hurt! Isn't that why this approach makes sense intellectually but rarely plays out in corporations? Losing face does not feel good. That's the point—it's Buckley's medicine for the corporate soul.

Head Versus Heart

Corporations and the people who run them tend to use a technical, data-based decision-making process that has no column in the spreadsheet to compute emotion. Their main assessment tool tends to be the extent of the danger of a hazard and how likely it is for the public to be hurt by their operations. In contrast, communities, as Sandman points out, tend toward emotional decision making. They value traits such as honesty, compassion, and fairness much more than technical competence, the main corporate driver. In other words, their emotional temperature is so high when they are outraged that the community will only accept information put forward by company experts if the community had a hand in picking them. This is less a battle over credentials, which is often how the company sees it, and more a question of power sharing—who gets to choose and who is shown the respect of being consulted.

Corporations' technical, data-based assessments are reinforced by their choice of advisers. When the corporate going gets tough, when the crisis is brewing, leaders turn to the people they use in non-critical times, who usually have huge self-interest and, unless specifically trained, a narrow focus. For example, lawyers are focused on winning in court, and engineers just want to do their pet project. Leaders should not expect dispassion and moderation from such partisan advisers. Although it's vital to consider these and other expert opinions, the role of the leader is to weigh the stakes and find the balance.

Vince Covello has outlined the leading corporate behaviors that often result from a technical decision-making focus, behaviors that fuel outrage:

- Don't involve communities in decisions.
- Hold on to information.
- Remain insensitive to people's feelings.
- Don't do what you promised.
- Deny glaring mistakes.
- Project arrogance and a negative attitude.
- Lie or make up information.
- Talk in jargon.
- Delay talking to the other side.
- Communicate through people who have nothing in common with the community and are insensitive to community members' concerns.

An example of avoiding the above pitfalls is the good work of BP in the aftermath of the Texas City refinery tragedy of March 2005, in which 15 people died and over 70 were injured. In that situation, care and concern drove all communications, and site management's public response was timely and focused on the emotional aspects of the incident. The head of BP worldwide, Lord John Browne, was on the scene within a day. Outreach programs were put in place. BP took complete responsibility and did what it could to ease the way forward for the families of those who were killed or injured. In addition, the company made public an extensive interim report outlining changes to its operations even before the official ruling came down. BP still has much work to do to restore trust, and any glitches during the rebuilding period will inevitably drag the company under the unforgiving glare of a global spotlight.

The tragedy of outrage management is that nothing about it is new. The concepts are as old as time itself. Indeed, Sandman refers to outrage management as the rules of the sandbox. But as a culture we seemed doomed to repeat the stereotypical mistakes on all sides, which run from a not-in-my-back-yard attitude, misinformation campaigns, unrealistic expectations, bribes, unintelligible data, flippant law suits, and buy offs. The usual result is that no one wins because the strategy was to get everything and leave the other side with nothing. This is a dangerous game, which I experienced as a young lawyer in Belfast in the 1980s, when the only outcomes under consideration were winning or losing. This philosophy contributed to my leaving in frustration.

Yet for corporations, it is tough to talk definitively about the effects of emissions from a new plant and answer long-term health questions. It's even tougher when community members don't want to hear the data until they feel that the corporation understands their concerns. But what corporations can uncover is what worries communities and then provide some perspective and context to that worry.

As we have discussed, the stark difference in decision-making style is a large part of the distrust between organizations and stakeholders. Communities will also point out that corporations' only reason to exist is to make money; their only allegiance, by law, is to shareholders. Corporations therefore have a strong financial interest in downplaying risk, as do their paid experts. One thing they will agree on is that one of the last things corporations ever want to do with communities is share power, and yet power is the most valuable currency in outrage management.

Of course sharing power is interesting in theory, but in practice this can be the toughest sell in the boardroom. Senior executives rarely achieve their positions by sharing much of anything. Many had sandbox-challenged childhoods. Their strategy is about competing, not collaborating; it's about winning, not sharing. In fact, they loathe sharing, but the smart ones realize that it gets them the coveted long-term license to operate.

When it comes to stakeholder relations, Consent = Respect + Skill. Our new leaders need to take the time to foster a culture of respect both inside and outside their corporations, a culture where a superior can be challenged and a neighbor may have a valid point. They need to build community action groups into each project's time line and budget. They must have mechanisms that allow the community to give feedback to corporate decision makers. They must take time to discover interests.

Furthermore, egos need to be managed. Losing face must be possible to achieve a higher goal, as must mediation before litigation—but without losing sight of the value of good old-fashioned negotiation, one-on-one over the proverbial kitchen table.

If we can get these actions in place, we'll be on our way to a healthy relationship between corporations and communities, one that is built on accountability, promises kept, listening, probing and understanding interests, and, above all, respect. Only then can we begin to restore some semblance of trust to our world.

On the CD-ROM

1 See *Biggest Challenges Organizations Face Today,* Christophe Roux-Dufort, "Zero Risk," and Ron Culp, "Deserving Trust."

2 See *Biggest Challenges Organizations Face Today,* Ron Culp, "Lack of Trust."

3 See *Creating a Crisis Leadership Culture,* Ron Culp, "Foster Trust."

4 See *Learning to Be a Crisis Leader,* Kathleen Sutcliffe, "Avoid Hubris."

CHAPTER 8

Framing Crisis Management: A Multiple Lens Perspective

by Lynn Perry Wooten

Lynn Perry Wooten is an assistant professor at University of Michigan's Ross School of Business, where she also earned her Ph.D. Her research focuses on sources of competitive advantages in organizations and how firms strategically adapt to changes in their labor markets. In addition, she studies strategic consequences of employee-centered crises and the effectiveness of diversity-management programs in organizations.

FOR EXECUTIVES, much of their formal training and on-the-job learning experiences emphasize the importance of the company's position, its competitors, consumer markets, and the value of collaborative partnerships. In many instances, however, these learning experiences neglect to address the importance of managing organizational crisis, even though executives are expected to take charge during a crisis situation. Without such learning, how can leaders develop a frame that serves as a reference point for understanding and preventing organizational crises?

Frames are lenses that bring the world into focus.[1] They can be built upon simple generalizations or complex theories and represent knowledge about a given concept. Frames filter organizational knowledge by helping managers make sense of experiences and provide a road map for decision making. Hence, frames are mental models that help organize leaders' thoughts and suggest appropriate action. Frames are powerful mental models because they reflect our view of the world and shape our behavior.[2]

Because of the nature of organizational crises, and the serious threats they pose, making sense of them requires framing through multiple lenses. Crises are often surprising and deceptive, the result of complex systems and environments filled with ambiguous information. Even when crises are not a surprise to management, the ramifications can be difficult to foresee. In a crisis situation, the behavior of organizational members is also more difficult to predict, and interactions among groups add to the complexity. During a crisis, stakeholders tend to provide incomplete information and try to camouflage mistakes. As a result of this complexity and ambiguity, managing becomes more important, but more difficult, during a crisis.

Drawing from organizational theory and management practice, I propose four frames that can help leaders manage crises. First is the strategic design frame, which explores the fit between an organization's strategy, structure, and the environment. Leaders viewing crises from the strategic design frame strive to resolve crises by bringing the organization back to a steady state, in which it can achieve efficiency and effectiveness. Second is the organizational politics frame, which considers organizational crises to be the result of power concentrated in the wrong places or too broadly dispersed, making crisis management a challenge. Third is the human resource frame. The fundamental assumption of this frame is that when managing crises, leaders should understand employees' capabilities and limitations. An additional perspective of this frame is that crises can escalate because of the prejudices, needs, and feelings of an organization's human capital. The fourth and final frame looks at crisis management through the lens of organizational culture. This frame views crises as a function of deeply ingrained values and rituals. Depending on the organizational setting, cultural values can prevent the organization from moving beyond crisis mode or provide the tools for doing so.

The next sections expand on the description of each frame and provide examples of how leaders can utilize them as crisis management tools.

Strategic Design

The strategic design perspective views organizations as systems constructed to achieve goals, and it assumes that the overarching goal is to create value for

**Thinking and Framing Crisis Management:
A Multiple Lens Perspective**

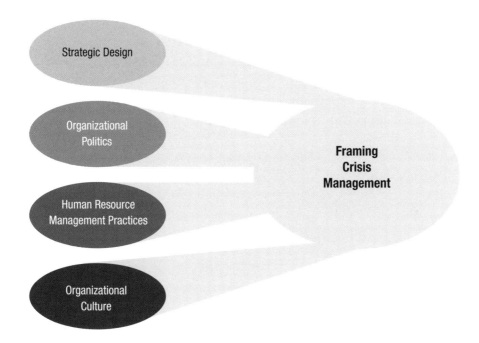

stakeholders.[3] Even in a crisis situation, the organization's value proposition serves as a guideline for deciding what activities management will implement to achieve its strategy. These patterns of decisions define objectives and result in plans for allocating and aligning resources to meet the needs of competitive pressures, customers, shareholders, and employees. Crafting strategies to minimize costs or provide a differentiated value to stakeholders is the essence of the strategic design approach.

Leaders framing the management of a crisis through a strategic design lens perceive the business world as rational and mechanistic. This mindset, which does not take into account the unexpected, prevents crisis preparation. When confronted with organizational crises, leaders' primary goal is to resolve the crisis and get back to "business as usual" as quickly as possible. In other words, management works to develop a strategy to bounce back from the crisis; but to overcome a crisis, the quest for resilience cannot contemplate only past mistakes.[4] Instead, an integral part of the strategic design frame assumes that after a crisis, leadership will concentrate on the future and shift its paradigm to restructure processes and resources.

For example, Martha Stewart Living Omnimedia (MSO) approached its management crisis from a strategic design frame. In March 2004, the firm's founder and CEO, Martha Stewart, was convicted of lying to investigators and conspiring with her stockbroker. In the temporary absence of its leader, the company had to reevaluate its dependency on a single person to market ideas, products, and services.[5] This resulted in changes to the administrative structure, a refocusing of the company's core competency, and contemplation about its future without Stewart. Confronted with this crisis, the firm's rhetoric and actions were orchestrated to convey to stakeholders that the company could not only survive but also continue to create value without Stewart. The communication strategy entailed sending a letter to shareholders, assuring them that the board of directors and employees were competent to manage the firm in her absence and that the "Martha" culture and way of doing things would persevere. The company's administrative team moved quickly to make the brand resilient by launching a food magazine and a natural lifestyle magazine that reflected Stewart's style, but these publications did not use her name, thus extending the brand beyond Martha Stewart's image. Also, domestic experts appeared on the television show and in *Living* magazine to substitute for Stewart.

The management of MSO's crisis reinforces the significance of thinking strategically about crises. Management at this company effectively established an action plan for surviving the crisis by minimizing the damage to the company's image and recreating its shareholders' value proposition.[6] Furthermore, the organization developed new strengths. All these strategic decisions resulted in a company that not only weathered the storm of a crisis, but in the long term is in a stronger competitive position.

Organizational Politics

Leaders often allocate a large proportion of their time to strategic planning and spend little time worrying about organizational politics. Many leaders perceive politics as the "dark side" of organizational life, constructed by the selfishness and dishonesty of others.[7] They do not want to play politics, and as result they become handicapped by their unwillingness to understand the role of politics in organizations.[8] Most organizational crises have a political aspect—politics can cause crises and be the means of resolving them.

Thus, thinking about organizational crises from a political frame is a necessary management skill. When leaders think about crises through this frame, they acknowledge that organizational behavior is not always deliberately constructed to achieve strategic goals. Instead, it can be dictated by conflicts among individuals, power structures, and competing interests. Framing crises from a political perspective requires in-depth knowledge of the organization's political terrain.[9] Leaders must be able to identify the strength of key power brokers, determine channels of communication, and understand networks of relationships. Moreover, when an organization's political system dominates business practices, leadership must comprehend how it creates crisis management barriers and then craft a plan to work around these obstacles. Not taking into account the political system can prolong the crisis and damage the organization.

Consider what happened to Arthur Andersen, the accounting firm that had been number one in its industry and known for excellent human resource management and client service practices. In 2002, this image was severely damaged when Arthur Andersen was accused of failing to detect fraud and report the improper accounting practices of firms such as Enron, WorldCom, Waste Management, and Sunbeam. The collapse of the firm represents a crisis rooted in a political system that leadership ignored.[10] In the previous decade, prior to the crisis, the firm's structure changed from a unified system to a loose confederation of fiefdoms intent on maximizing billable hours. As the fiefdoms grew, so did power struggles within and between local offices. The power brokers were the partners who increased revenues at the expense of quality, retaining high-risk clients with questionable accounting practices. Partners at Arthur Andersen speaking against these practices were removed from the firm's oversight committee. In addition, the power brokers developed a system to ensure that the top management team never received detailed information about problem clients.

The Arthur Andersen crisis emphasizes not only the importance of leadership's role in understanding the organization's political terrain but also the significance of leaders' ability to navigate organizational politics. Joseph Berardino, worldwide CEO of Arthur Andersen at the time of the scandal, had inherited a crisis-prone political system, but he was unable to comprehend the complexity of the problem. He needed to understand the reality of the political system and correct that system to protect the firm. Preventing and managing crises through a political system requires an ability to build healthy networks, negotiate with power brokers, and refocus the values of the dominant coalition when it jeopardizes the organization's well-being.

Human Resource Management Practices

Like the organizational politics frame, the human resource frame directs leaders to think about the "people" side of crisis management—more specifically, the relationship between an organization's employees and a crisis. An organization and its employees exist in a relationship of mutual exchange, in which they interact not only with each other but also with the economic environment, demographic patterns, and socio-cultural trends.[11] Organizations need employees for their talents and ideas. Employees need employers to provide monetary rewards, meet their affiliation needs, and allow them to achieve self-actualization. An imbalance between organizational goals and employees' needs can produce a crisis.

Frequently, such imbalances are the result of human resource management practices, such as discriminatory behavior in the workplace and union disputes. In 2003, the Institute for Crisis Management estimated that crises resulting from discriminatory practices increased by 110 percent over the previous year, and combined labor disputes and employee discrimination accounted for 14 percent of business crises. Yet, executives seldom make the connection between business crises and the organization's human resource management practices.[12] Executives are more likely to blame employees.

Consider Wal-Mart, which has been accused of discriminating against women, ethnic minorities, and disabled employees. For years Wal-Mart denied there were problems with its human resource management practices, despite the fact that the company was losing lawsuits and receiving negative media attention. Wal-Mart's denial of the crisis placed it substantially behind in the diversity-management learning curve.[13] Now the retailer is spending money to rectify its human resource practices and restore its image.

Labor disputes can also send an organization into crisis. General Motors cites the cost of health care benefits negotiated by the union as one reason for the company's current financial problems and competitive disadvantage. Employees expect a certain level of health benefits, but the rising costs of these benefits conflict with shareholders' goals. External factors can cause an employee-centered crisis because of disparities in labor markets or economic conditions. Labor shortages in certain industrial sectors illustrate crises resulting from human resource management imbalances. For example, the labor shortages in nursing have created a crisis for hospitals.[14] Fewer college students are choosing nursing as a career, while many veteran nurses are retiring or leaving the profession because of working conditions. This shortage threatens the quality of patient care and the ability of hospitals to serve communities, which are demanding increased health-care services. However, most hospitals did not exercise the foresight that could have helped prevent this crisis. In the 1990s, managed health-care policies led to the downsizing of the nursing workforce without regard for maintaining a pipeline of nurses for the future. Nurses remaining in the field experienced stressful work environments with mandatory overtime. The industry is now being forced to solve the nursing shortage through public relations campaigns, partnering with nursing schools, innovative recruitment and retention policies, and flexible work arrangements.

When dealing with crises grounded in human resource management practices, leaders should reflect on how the organization can change its routines to achieve balance between the organization and its employees. This entails creating a work environment where the needs of employees are not neglected and are aligned with the organization's goals. Environments in which labor and management work as partners to achieve the organization's mission can go a long way toward achieving this balance. Avoiding employee-centered crises also calls for careful forecasting of labor needs and macro-environment trends.

Organizational Culture

Culture is the glue that holds people in organizations together. Organizational culture provides direction and purpose, and defines what is appreciated and rewarded. Because of its unique and valuable attributes, an organization's culture designed specifically to manage crisis can be a useful asset. A crisis situation heightens anxiety, but when organizations have a culture prepared to manage and learn from the crisis, the resolution will be less difficult.[15]

There are some lessons to be learned from organizations that are in the business of crisis management, such as the Red Cross and Doctors Without Borders. In these organizations, norms and work procedures facilitate crisis management. Leaders are ready to help when a crisis strikes. Their mindset is explicit in the organization's mission and ingrained in how its executives utilize financial resources and mobilize staff. More important, organizations in the crisis management business value learning from crisis incidents. Explicit learning is documented in policy manuals, and tacit learning is incorporated into the organization's culture. Hence, each crisis incident develops into a potential opportunity for cultural renewal if leadership reflects on the exposed weaknesses and creates new managerial practices.

Conclusion

The four frames described here are not intended to be stand-alone perspectives. Because the frames complement one another, leaders should integrate them for the most effective crisis management. When executives use the frames as tools, they move beyond the firing-squad mentality to become thought leaders. The strategic design frames encourages leaders to develop an action plan for bouncing back from

Framing Crisis Management

Framing Lens	Crisis Management Actions
Strategic Design	Resolve the crisis by returning organization to a steady state. Craft future strategic plans to build resilience. Develop new strengths to compensate for weaknesses exposed during the crisis. Implement an action plan to address the concerns of stakeholders. Shift managerial paradigm to restructure processes and resources.
Organizational Politics	Map the organization's political terrain. Determine if the organization's political system is a crisis hazard. Identify power brokers and assess their role in the crisis. Develop networks of supporters to help manage the crisis. Refocus the values of the dominant coalition.
Human Resource Management Practices	Understand the link between business crises and human resource management practices. Analyze the capabilities and limitations of the organization's human capital. Evaluate any imbalance between the organization's goals and its employees' needs. Assess if discriminatory work practices, labor shortages, or labor disputes make the organization susceptible to a crisis. Scan the external environment for conditions that could threaten the organization's human-resource-management needs.
Organizational Culture	Develop a culture prepared to manage crises. Remove cultural barriers that contribute to crises. Craft a mission and practice symbolic behavior to lead organizational members through a crisis. Leverage crisis situations to renew organizational culture.

crises that takes into account the needs of various stakeholders. This action plan should analyze the organization's post-crisis position in the marketplace to minimize its weaknesses and rebuild its strengths. Framing a crisis through an organizational politics lens also requires managerial analysis. However, the focal point of this analysis is mapping networks and identifying power brokers with the goal of mitigating negative energy in the political system. Similar to the organizational politics frame, the human resource management perspective emphasizes the importance of a strategy for realigning the organization's goals with the needs of its employees and the labor market environment. Lastly, the organizational culture frame serves as a lens for transforming an organization from crisis-prone to crisis-prepared. It urges leaders to build a culture that is prepared for crisis and excels at adapting quickly to crisis situations.[16] This is accomplished through an integrated set of shared values, tacit norms, and explicit work procedures that promote flexibility, resourcefulness, and responsiveness during a crisis.

Framing organizational crises through multiple lenses is a new mental model and a new tool. Well-prepared and capable managers are able to look through all four frames when managing a crisis. Moreover, these leaders have the ability to be both reflective and forward thinking about crisis situations. As a result, a crisis that initially threatens an organization may, in the long term, give leaders the opportunity to rebuild and renew their organizations.

---

1. L. Bolman and T. Deal, *Reframing Organizations: Artistry, Choice, and Leadership* (San Francisco: Jossey-Bass, 1991).

2. P. Senge, "Mental Models: Putting Strategic Ideas into Practice," *Planning Review* 20 (1992): 4-11.

3. D. Ancona, T. Kochan, M. Scully, J. Van Mannen, and E. Westney, *Managing for the Future: Organizational Behavior and Processes,* New York Southwestern College.

4. G. Hamel and L. Valikangas, "The Quest for Resilience," *Harvard Business Review,* Sept. 2003: 52-65.

5. C. Hays, "As Stewart Enters Prison, Her Company Refurbishes," *New York Times,* October 8, 2004, C4.

6. A. Lum and D. Lum, "Martha Stewart: What's In a Name?" *Business & Economic Review* 51 (2005): 13-16.

7. Ancona et al., *Managing for the Future.*

8. J. Pffefer, *Managing With Power: Politics and Influence in Organizations* (Boston: Harvard Business School Press, 1994).

9. Bolman and Deal, *Reframing Organizations.*

10. J. Byrne, "Joe Berardino's Fall from Grace," *BusinessWeek,* August 12, 2002: 52.

11. P. Bamberger and I. Meshoulam, *Human Resource Strategy* (Thousand Oaks, California: Sage Publications, 2000).

12. L. Wooten and L. James, "When Firms Fail to Learn: The Perpetuation of Discrimination in the Workplace," *Journal of Management Inquiry* 13(1): 23-33.

13. L. Bean, "Wal-Mart Diversity Head: Can't Back Claims with Numbers," DiversityInc, August-September, 2004, 22.

14. United Nurses of America (2005). Nursing shortage. http://www.afscme.org/una/sns04.htm.

15. E. James and L. Wooten, "Leadership as (Un)usual: How to Display Competence in Times of Crisis," *Organizational Dynamics* 34 (2) (2005): 141-152.

16. M. Valle, "Crisis, Culture and Charisma: The New Leader's Work in Public Organization," *Public Personnel Management* 28 (2) (1999): 245-257.

On the CD-ROM

1 See *Biggest Challenges Organizations Face Today,* Christophe Roux-Dufort, "Expect Perfection."

2 See *Biggest Challenges Organizations Face Today,* Christophe Roux-Dufort, "View Crisis as a Process."

3 See *Learning to Be a Crisis Leader,* David Shapiro, "Be Skeptical."

4 See *Learning to Be a Crisis Leader,* Bill McCloskey, "Own Your Mistakes."

5 See *Learning to Be a Crisis Leader,* Bill McCloskey, "Understand Processes."

Crisis Leadership in Action

CHAPTER 9

The Case of Cebu Pacific Air

by Marie-Grace U. Ngo with James G. Clawson and Gerry Yemen

Commentary
by Gerry Yemen

FEBRUARY 2, 1998, WAS ANOTHER busy morning for Lance Gokongwei, the 31-year-old chief executive officer of Cebu Pacific Air (Cebu). Seated at the boardroom table, Gokongwei was about to start his regular meeting with the food business division when the telephone rang. On the other end was Cebu's operations head, Diego Garrido, with disturbing news. Flight 5J-387 from Manila to Cagayan de Oro failed to arrive at its destination on schedule and was believed to be missing. Filled with disbelief, Gokongwei abruptly ended his meeting and proceeded to the Cebu offices in Mandaluyong. While he hoped that there had been a mistake in the information, the first question that filled the young CEO's mind was "Could this be true?"

The safety of the crew members and passengers was Gokongwei's deepest concern. The airline was barely three years old and just beginning to gain significant market presence in the Philippine domestic airline industry. How would a plane crash affect the company and its employees? Was the airline negligent, and therefore was he, as CEO, personally responsible for the accident?

Cebu Pacific Air

Shortly after deregulation of the Philippine aviation industry in 1995, Cebu Pacific Air was one of the three major airlines launched in that country. The company's single biggest stockholder, JG Summit Holdings (JGS), owned 49 percent of the airline.[1]

In January 1998, the company utilized a fleet of eight DC9-32 McDonnell Douglas aircraft, with an all-coach 110/115 seating capacity and a 32-inch seat pitch. Cebu adopted the maintenance program of the Philippine Air Transportation Office, which included high standards for recruitment, training, and recurrent training of mechanics; maintenance of adequate parts inventory and of tools and equipment; and purchase, shipment, monitoring, and replacement of parts, tools, and equipment. A quality control inspector supervised all inspections, and a quality assurance inspector conducted all spot-checks. Eight mechanics conducted night-stop inspections on each aircraft from nose to wingtip to tail.

From the outset, Cebu boasted a focused strategy and a narrowly defined niche. The airline flew point to point, had a very simple fare structure, and operated only one type of aircraft. Consequently, operating costs were relatively low, and Cebu passed on its savings to customers. Within two years, the company had flown 1.5 million passengers. By February 1998, Cebu's load factor, or seat occupancy rate, was in the high 80s, compared with the industry leader's low 70s. Cebu's on-time performance was in the high 90s. The company's 34 percent market share in its routes meant Cebu had managed to become the second-largest airline in the country.

Lance Gokongwei

Lance Gokongwei, son of JG Summit founder John Gokongwei, was named president and CEO of Cebu Pacific Air from the carrier's inception in March 1996. Gokongwei intended to make Cebu the "Filipino's airline of choice"; the company's mission was to become "the low-fare, great value airline." He envisioned a company that the public trusted to be a vital partner in the nation's progress. To instill this mission in each employee, Gokongwei created a team-driven environment that became the firm's fundamental advantage. He moved away from tradition and instituted a flat corporate structure where bureaucracy was kept to a minimum. Profit-sharing plans and an open door policy were used to encourage employees to take a personal stake in the company. Gokongwei created a corporate environment where employees were able to propose ideas freely and directly to senior management with full knowledge that they would be heard. Gokongwei stressed the need to build a high-trust environment to keep communication lines open and information flowing. For example, two flight attendants approached Gokongwei about a routinely malfunctioning toilet. Immediately he had it fixed and from then on focused more on customers' comfort.

Gokongwei guarded the airline's team spirit with diligence. Group interviews and psychological profiles reinforced the recruitment process. He believed in spending amply on employee training not only in technical skills but also in team building, values clarification, and behavioral workshops. As a result, employees displayed outstanding work habits. While general domestic industry standards required an average of 20 people at an airport to perform ground tasks like check-in, ticket sales, and baggage services, Cebu managed well with fewer than half that number.[2] The commitment Cebu made to its employees resulted in a team-driven work environment fully committed to serving customers. When interviewed, Cebu passengers stressed their satisfaction with the quality and fun-filled experience of the airline's in-flight service in addition to low airfares.

The Accident

Flight 5J-387 was a direct flight from Manila to Lumbia Airport, Cagayan de Oro. But on February 2, 1998, flight 5J-387 made a planned technical stop at Tacloban to transport personnel and equipment for another aircraft grounded with a flat tire. The technical stop was intended to minimize a six-hour delay for passengers on the Tacloban to Manila flight as well as all other flights that were scheduled to use the same aircraft that day.

Flight 5J-387 had 99 passengers on board and five crew members when it left Manila at 9 A.M. The plane arrived in Tacloban at 10:02 A.M. and departed for Cagayan de Oro at 10:20, scheduled to arrive at 11. At 10:42, the Air Transportation Office (ATO) controller cleared the flight to proceed off airways Butuan and to descend to traffic altitude upon leaving the airways.[3] At 10:44, the flight reported that they were overhead Butuan, so the Cagayan de Oro Approach Control cleared the flight to proceed off airways.[4] The last radio contact with flight 5J-387 was at 10:48, advising Cagayan de Oro Airport control of the start of descent. The pilot reported that he was 68 kilometers (42 miles) from the airport at an altitude of 11,500 feet. Estimated time of arrival was 11:03. That was the last communication from flight 5J-387.

Twelve hours later, at 10 P.M., flight 5J-387 was yet to be found. Gokongwei and his staff had no information for victims' families or leads from which they could begin any rescue efforts. At the same time, there was mounting pressure from the media to release a statement. On national television, victims' families expressed growing frustration with the company. The media reported various stories on the radio, television, and newspapers. Amidst all the uncertainty and noise, the Philippine government, swayed significantly by public opinion, was under pressure to take some action. There were talks of possible airline grounding.

As Gokongwei took in the complexity of the situation, he realized that the company's image and culture of caring and openness, factors he believed were the firm's competitive advantages, were at stake. He considered the firm's moral obligation to support the ATO in search and rescue operations. He needed to think about Cebu's priorities during this chaotic period and to implement a plan of action to fulfill them. With the stigma of this experience hanging in the air, would it be possible for the company to continue providing a work environment that employees could be proud of? Would Cebu be able to count on the support of the Filipino public? Gokongwei reflected on how he should deal with the current situation and its aftermath—with his employees, the victims' families, the governmental authority, and the media.

As the reality of the tragedy sank in, Gokongwei led his management team to focus on facing up to the problem. The company acted on its commitment to behave like a responsible corporate citizen even if it meant going beyond the bounds of legal obligations. For instance, Cebu strove to maintain the highest level of transparency with the media and the government. Realizing the importance of meeting the needs of victims' families, corporate priorities were turned toward helping with search and rescue operations, then assisting the families, followed by cooperating with the authorities in their investigation.

Search and Rescue Operations

Cebu was fully involved in the search and rescue operations of the Presidential Action Center that Philippine president Ramos organized and former congressman Jesus Dureza headed. The company dispatched two helicopters for additional use by the search and rescue teams headed by the Philippine Armed Forces. They also provided rescuers with food and supplies.

Public pressure mounted with every hour the Cebu jet remained missing. The media broadcast erroneous claims that a crash site was discovered in the mountains and that 15 survivors were sighted. A mayor from a nearby town confirmed the reports. At the same time, Gokongwei was criticized for refusing to confirm the jet had crashed and been spotted. The frantic search for the missing Cebu flight included bizarre political considerations. A group of anti-government guerrilla fighters, native to the mountainous area where the jet was thought to be, offered to help with the search. The Philippine military removed a well-known television station's cameraman from the search area. Journalists reported the government had kidnapped their cameraman and demanded his release. Shortly thereafter the young man returned to the television station. All of these incidents made top billing in media coverage.

Finally on February 3, positive sightings of flight 5J-387 were confirmed at 10:00 A.M. The wreck was along Mt. Lumot, Sumagaya Range, in Claveria, a town in the city of Misamis Oriental at an altitude of 6,920 feet. As search and rescue operations continued, hope that anyone survived the ill-fated crash diminished. Instead, more and more body bags filled with human remains were transported to the National Power Corporation hangar, where a mortuary was set up and forensic experts were stationed to identify the passengers. Acknowledging the need to bring in more experienced forensic experts, Cebu contracted the services of Global Partners Ltd. to work with the National Bureau of Investigation's forensics team in the recovery and identification of passengers.[5]

Cebu's Image Under Threat

From the first report that one of Cebu's flights was unaccounted for, the company faced constant attacks about the age and safety of its aircraft—the DC9-32. In response, Cebu asserted that the airworthiness of the plane was beyond question. Company and ATO records confirmed that the plane was last inspected for BO3 check on December 29, 1997.[6] As of February 2, 1998, the plane used for flight 5J-387 had 97 flight-hours remaining before its next D check. The next forecasted major check or complete aircraft overhaul was due in 2002. The aircraft had 12, 948 remaining flight-hours before the check.

The airline was criticized for an alleged illegal diversion of what was supposedly a direct flight from Manila to Cagayan de Oro. The stop to Tacloban City was announced at the check-in counter, the predeparture area, and during the preflight announcement when the passengers were on board.

Opponents argued that had it not been for the route change, the pilots on flight 5J-387 would not have had to fly over an unfamiliar airway. The so-called Tacloban City "diversion" was neither illegal nor irregular. Instead, it was a planned flight, approved by the ATO, in accordance with its established procedures and policies. Two flight plans were prepared. The flight plan for the first segment was signed by the captain in command and a representative of the ATO in Manila. The second segment was relayed to the ATO in Tacloban through the Cebu office there. In addition, the flight deck crew was briefed on the weather and terrain on both routes.

The reputation of the flight crew was also at stake. Captain Paolo Maria C. Justo, Cebu's pilot in command on flight 5J-387, and co-pilot, First Officer Erwin U. Golla, were experienced, decorated, and well-trained pilots. Captain Justo trained in the Philippine Air Force (PAF) flying school in 1989. In August 1996, he trained at the Northwest Aerospace Training Center in Minnesota and was rated to fly DC9 jets. Justo had a total flying time of 4,052 hours, 751 of which were on the DC9. In 1985, First Officer Golla was trained in the PAF flying school. He was rated on the DC9 during May 1997 after being trained at the Flight Safety International Airline Training Center in Florida. Golla had a total flying time of 2,450 hours, 163 of which were on the DC9.

The integrity of the company was under close scrutiny as it faced attacks that involved the airworthiness of the aircraft, the legality of a diversion to another city, and pilot incompetence.

Helping Victims' Families

The Cebu management team organized support services that provided families and the general public with updated information. This information cost the company an average of PHP2 million per day. The airline also provided family members with transportation to and from Cagayan de Oro, as well as meals and accommodations. Gokongwei personally set up a command post that coordinated all necessary assistance and services to immediate family members of the passengers. A central administration team was formed in Manila and a counterpart team in Cagayan de Oro. These teams comprised senior managers and 150 other Cebu personnel. According to a victim's son, senior management was there to provide support each day. Cebu employees, each of whom was assigned to one family, developed a personal relationship with the victims' families. Meanwhile, at a 24-hour coordinating and communications center in Manila, employees answered phones and provided updates to the media, hoping to meet the Filipino people's demand for more accurate and timely information.

The company made a conscious effort to ensure that the victims' families were closely cared for throughout the ordeal. Briefing sessions were held at the Dynasty Hotel in Cagayan de Oro each day, which informed families of the latest news before the information was given to the media for public release. In addition to the compensation due the victims' families in accordance with Philippine law, Cebu offered financial assistance to cover funeral and burial expenses to all families. Because no one at the company had experience in Islamic practices, it offered these families a lump sum to arrange services in keeping with their faith.

Authorities' Inquiries

In a press conference on February 4, 1998, President Ramos stated that the ATO must ground the airline as a matter of standard operating procedure. Not everyone agreed with the policy; ATO safety division chief Saturnino de la Cruz had announced earlier that he ruled out engine malfunction. Despite Cruz's findings, on February 5 the ATO declared the grounding and suspension of Cebu's flight operations. Management accepted this decision and cooperated fully in the investigation that ATO chief Carlos Tanega conducted.

Gokongwei and the rest of his management team were confident that Cebu was fully compliant with all legal and safety requirements and would fly again soon. But employees down the line were uncertain about the airline's future. Their jobs, families, and careers were at stake. On the day the airline was grounded, Gokongwei wrote a letter to all employees describing what was going on and what the company had planned. He emphasized his continued commitment to the airline, its mission, and the employees. Gokongwei further expressed hope that they would show the general public the Cebu spirit of service and teamwork—factors that he considered responsible for the company's past two years of success.

After the tragic ending to flight 5J-387, Cebu's transparency with the media, full cooperation with the government, assistance to victims' families at a personal level, and readiness to face up to its obligations gained the sympathy and trust of the public. Statements were published in national newspapers that expressed confidence in the airworthiness of Cebu and disapproval of the airline's suspension. More important, Gokongwei received encouragement and support from his employees through their volunteer efforts during the disaster and letters of support, while hundreds took unpaid leaves.[7]

Nearly half of the Cebu staff in Manila volunteered to be stationed in Cagayan de Oro to assist the search and rescue operations as well as to comfort the victims' families. Some stayed on the mountain through the night while others assisted in the morgues. The most notable contribution that Cebu employees made to the victims' families was the "gabay" system.[8] Each volunteer was assigned to a family to act as their coordinator, liaison, caregiver, gofer, and friend. They took customer care several steps further, as each employee worked one-on-one with the families to meet their needs, offered a shoulder to lean on, and shared a bit of the burden. Bonds were formed and a deep feeling of loss was shared among everyone. Senior Vice President and General Manager Diego Garrido, one of the volunteers, was reportedly unable to temper his own grief and was quoted as saying, "If I could give my life in exchange for your relatives, I would gladly do so." As mentioned in a volunteer's account, their dedication to the families was an expression of loyalty to the company—but, more to the point, stemmed from a genuine commitment to serve. Cebu management supported volunteers, worked alongside them, commiserated with them, and requested the assistance of psychologists from the Department of Health and the Department of Social Welfare and Development.

Through the company's management of this tragic incident, Cebu gained public respect for its outstanding corporate citizenship. Throughout the experience, the firm showed its dedication to passenger welfare through its sincere efforts to care for the needs of the families. Compassion was exhibited throughout the organization—from senior management to the rank and file.

On February 9, 1998, the flight data recorder from flight 5J-387 was found and turned over to the ATO investigation team. Unfortunately, the recorder was badly damaged and unreadable. The following day, the ground warning positioning system device (GWPSD) was recovered within the vicinity of the crash site. Investigators discovered that the GWPSD had been activated prior to the impact and had warned the pilot to pull up because of the jet's close proximity to the terrain. The cockpit voice recorder (CVR) was finally recovered at the crash site on February 14, and the following transcript was discovered:

10:49:28 A.M.
CAM 2 (F.O. Golla, co-pilot)
"Don't you think there are mountains there?"

10:49:30 A.M.
CAM 2 (Capt. Justo, pilot)
"Maybe there is none."

10:49:46 A.M.
CAM 2 (F.O. Golla, co-pilot)
"Leveling off at five thousand feet, sir."

10:49:48 A.M.
CAM 2 (Capt. Justo, pilot)
"O.K., sir."

10:49:50 A.M.
CAM 2 (F.O. Golla, co-pilot)
"I cannot see anything just to make sure."

10:49:57 A.M.
GPWS begins squawking the warning: *"Terrain, terrain…"*
CAM 2 (F.O. Golla, co-pilot)
"There it is!"

10:49:58 A.M.
Panel warning system starts sounding: *"Whoop, whoop… pull up."*
(This is repeated for 13 seconds).

10:50:12 A.M.
After a final *"Whoop,"* the recording comes to an end.

After 60 days, the ATO lifted the ban that grounded the airline, effective on April 1, 1998. Authorities disclosed that pilot error caused the crash of Cebu flight 5J-387 and concluded that the airline had complied with all preflight requirements. Some requirements were imposed prior to resuming all flights. For instance, all Cebu pilots had to undergo a retraining program and pass a proficiency check in the United States. The company's operations, procedures, airplanes, and equipment underwent a full audit prior to the resumption of operations on April 6, 1998. In September 1998, the ATO conducted a stringent aviation safety audit for all airlines—and Cebu passed. Airplanes from three other airlines were grounded for noncompliance with safety standards.

Meanwhile, the licensing authority, ATO, came under fire. There were criticisms regarding its aircraft inspection policies. Allegations were made that there was a gross lack of human resources—28 inspectors were responsible for the 800 aircraft that flew within the country; only eight ATO pilots were expected to monitor the country's 818 pilots.

The authorities were also criticized over the location of Cagayan de Oro's Lumbia Airport. There were no airways between Butuan and Cagayan de Oro, and the airport facilities in Cagayan de Oro failed to keep up with progress. Pilots used visual flight rules on this flight path. The National Power Corporation and the Cagayan de Oro Electric Power & Light Company's power lines interfered with the operation of instrument landing systems. ATO authorities were aware of the danger the mountain range posed on this flight path, which was characterized by thick clouds and air turbulence. Within the past four years, five airplanes had crashed in the same location. Plans to build a new airport in Laguindingan, Misamis Oriental, had existed since 1993. The proposed coastal flight path was safer for both ascending and descending air traffic. Yet nothing past the planning stage had developed.

Over the two months that its operations were grounded, Cebu incurred approximately PHP70 million in losses. No one in the Cebu family resigned as a result of the crisis. On the first month of resumption, Cebu's load factor averaged a high 79 percent, and on-time performance was an outstanding 95 percent. As of August 1999, the airline had carried almost four million passengers, and revenues were expected to reach PHP3 billion.

The Cebu Pacific culture that Gokongwei envisioned was characterized by a deep sense of family, and caring for the company and colleagues was exhibited through the employees' volunteer efforts in this tragedy. Gokongwei received encouragement and support from his employees, while hundreds took unpaid leaves.[9] Years after the tragedy, the company continued to care for the families of the victims. Cebu provided transportation to Cagayan de Oro on important days like birthdays, death anniversaries, and All Saints' Day.[10] Gokongwei recalled, "While I deeply regret the loss of lives, some good came from the experience. It strengthened my belief that my job is not just to run a company for myself but for everyone who contributes to it."[11]

Commentary

The situation that Lance Gokongwei, CEO of Cebu Pacific Air, faced is an example of one of the sudden crises that account for 29 percent of all business crises annually. As Larry Smith explains in chapter one, this company needs three plans—operations, crisis communication, and business recovery—to pull through the disaster quickly. While the case doesn't explicitly mention the existence of a crisis response plan, Gokongwei did quickly bring together senior executives, suggesting this step was part of the company's emergency plan. The first few hours after the accident left the impression, however, that a crisis communication plan, if the airline had one, was slow to emerge.

Although the plane crash was a sudden crisis for the victims' families and friends—as well as for the airline—there may have been smoldering organizational issues in the company that contributed to the disaster. For instance, was this crisis the result of a strategic design that was meant to minimize costs, as Lynn Wooten describes in chapter eight? Applying a strategic design perspective, we can consider a number of issues. For example, the potential misalignment between the original strategic structure and the environment cannot be ignored. Nor can the rate at which the company grew. The attitude seemed to be that the airline could do more with less, which resulted in using second-hand DC9-32 aircrafts and running ground operations with fewer employees than the rest of the industry. It is conceivable that in an effort to grow quickly, the company took inappropriate measures that compromised safety.

Examining the organizational structure and human resource practices may also be fruitful. The company culture of fun may have detracted from the serious side of taking care of business. Perhaps the organizational design lacked control; the structure was too flat. An argument could be made that organizational behavior was distracted by the power structures. With chains of command harder to define, there may have been some confusion over where in the organization important decisions were made. At 31 years old, Gokongwei might have lacked the appropriate leadership skills to run an airline. Did he have too much faith in his employees? Had the firm made hiring mistakes? Were employee training and development adequate? All these variables matter—particularly when the stakes are high.

To sort through these complex issues and determine what we would do if leading Cebu through this crisis, we could start by identifying the stakeholders: victims' families, employees, Cebu ticket holders, future customers, the media, the government, and regulatory bodies. Once the stakeholders have been identified, we can assess which group will need a response from Gokongwei first and what their needs may be. A key leadership issue in this task is to recognize stakeholders' needs and make appropriate decisions when these needs are competing for limited organizational resources.

Each constituency is interested in what Gokongwei will do and each may be adversarial, ambivalent, or an advocate for Gokongwei and Cebu. As Timothy Coombs suggests in chapter four, we should anticipate how various stakeholders will react to the situation and discuss what type of response may be appropriate for each group. For example, adversaries (who may have the potential to further threaten or harm the organization) and advocates (who may have the potential to help or support the organization) should perhaps receive priority status. Yet we learn in the case that 12 hours after the crash, neither the victims' families nor the public had heard anything from Gokongwei. Family members expressed their outrage and sorrow through various media outlets.

We could ask whether the CEO panicked. Was Gokongwei exhibiting the "stunned, seemingly frozen, deer in the headlights" response that Mary Waller outlines in chapter six? Given the fact that crashes are not unheard of in the airline industry, and that other planes had crashed in these very mountains, did the outwardly slow reaction from Cebu mean that its leader panicked or that the airline had no crisis plan?

In the first few hours following the crash, the intense media scrutiny and speculation about the tragedy put more pressure on Cebu executives and the Philippine government to respond. Gokongwei fell short in his initial actions and the government grounded the entire airline in response to the outcry from victims' families. When he finally does publicly address the crisis, what should Gokongwei say to the various stakeholders? If Gokongwei took a leadership role, a comprehensive response plan would include a description of what the airline intends to do in response to the crisis. This "action" piece of the organization's strategy should include a management response, an operational response, and a communication response.

Crisis Management or Crisis Leadership? In chapter two, Christine Pearson makes clear that one of the key points of leading through a crisis is "doing the right thing." Did Gokongwei do the right thing? In a crisis such as this, the needs of the victims' families must be a priority. After seemingly dragging their feet in the first few hours, the airline's executives jumped into action. The company made meeting the needs of victims' families a priority. Senior managers focused on search and rescue operations until they learned the sad fate of passengers. Then the company assisted and comforted families, providing transportation, meals, and accommodations. The one-on-one contact between airline employees and victims' family members developed into very personal relationships.

Garth Rowan writes in chapter seven that the goal for managing stakeholders is to maintain their loyalty—their consent to keep doing business—through respect and a good safety track record. This formula helps corporate leaders avoid public outrage. From a safety point of view, the company immediately asserted the airworthiness of its equipment and use of experienced pilots. And technically, they were correct. Cebu passed standard government safety tests and hired well-trained pilots. In spite of that, a truly tragic event unfolded. Once Gokongwei focused on the emotional aspects of the accident, victims' families and public attitudes toward the company changed. Indeed, we learn that Gokongwei and Cebu had fostered a culture of respect both inside and outside the company. When the government grounded the rest of the airline's fleet, the public and employees stepped forward to show support for the young CEO and his company.

At the end of the case, we discover that pilot error caused the accident. We also learn that while operations were shut down, hundreds of employees took unpaid leaves, volunteered to act as "shepherds" for victims' families, and sent Gokongwei letters of support. Bonds were formed, and a deep feeling of loss was shared. Not a single employee quit as a result of the crash. To a large extent can we attribute the results of Gokongwei's crisis handling to the company culture that he created. In times of crisis, he was able to draw on this culture as a means of supporting the organization.

While we don't learn from the case whether Gokongwei apologized, his crisis plan went beyond the company's legal obligations. This also can be credited to the attention to company culture that Gokongwei had nurtured during the previous two years. He listened to employees, invested in training, and diligently guarded team spirit. During this very difficult time, Gokongwei lived up to Cebu's mission to provide genuine service and support to its customers. Gokongwei took care of the financial and emotional needs of victims' families and showed that they were not alone in this tragedy. Most important, the culture Gokongwei envisioned, characterized by a deep sense of family and caring for the company and colleagues, was exhibited through employees' volunteer efforts. While under a spotlight, this young CEO drew upon leadership competencies that Erika James discusses in chapter three: embodying trust, adopting an inclusive mindset, and taking the lead with actions that represent a desire to do the right thing.

In Another Context. To what extent would the airline's crisis plan and priorities have been different, given a different cultural and economic environment? Gokongwei's actions reflect the value system of the Filipino people. If this were to happen in the United States, the legal aspect would probably play a much larger role in how the incident would be handled. The authorities may not have needed help from the company in search and rescue efforts or forensic investigations. The company may not have felt as much pressure to consider their moral and societal obligations. Operating effectively in global business environments, especially during crises, means advance thinking about cross-cultural differences.

After the Tragedy. The Cebu airline crash in the Philippines was an emotional event that touched many lives. As a result of this disaster, the airline lost approximately PHP70 million in revenue. Six months later, the regulatory authority conducted rigorous safety audits for all airlines and discovered noncompliance in three Philippine airlines (Cebu passed). Even though Cebu was unprepared for this disaster and made mistakes (most noticeably the lack of a crisis communication plan), the culture Gokongwei nurtured within the company, and ultimately adopted to deal with the crisis, helped this company retain employees, customers, and public support. Gokongwei believed the culture of caring and openness was the firm's competitive advantage. Fortunately he adopted the strategy as a guide in the airline's response to the crash. Seven years later, the airline continues its on-time performance and remains the second-largest airline in the Philippines. For years after the accident, the company continued to care for victims' families and provide transportation to the crash site during important memorial days.

---

1. JGS, with 1998 gross revenues of PHP27 billion (approximately US$675 million) was one of the Philippines' biggest and most diversified holding companies with businesses involving food, banking, real estate, hotels, textiles, telecommunications, petrochemicals, cement, and power generation. JGS promised Cebu firm financial support up to PHP2 billion (US$50 million).

2. Alexandra Seno, *AsiaWeek,* October 8, 1999.

3. Airways are like invisible highways in the sky, with route numbers and rules for flying on them, between navigational beacons. If the pilot is a civilian in a small plane (General Aviation) below 18,000 feet and can see for certain minimum distances, he or she is allowed to fly in accordance with Visual Flight Rules (VFRs). This can be either on or off an airway. If pilots want to allow a ground controller to navigate the route of flight and altitude, then the craft proceeds under Instrument Flight Rules (IFRs). Flying IFR is mandatory above 18,000 feet or in bad weather, and at all times in any weather for passenger and military aircraft, except when the aircraft is in visual range of an airport. Depending on the navigational equipment in the airplane and the ground controller's desires, pilots can fly either on or off an airway.

In this case, when the aircraft reported it was over the Butuan navigational point, the controller cleared the plane to get off the airway and fly directly to the Cagayan de Oro Airport while still under IFR rules.

4. Civil Aeronautics Board, Accident Report.

5. Global Partners Ltd. (DVI) is an international emergency investigation team based in the United Kingdom, specializing in disaster victim identification.

6. BO3 checks include A, B, and C checks. BO4 checks include A, B, C, and D checks.

A check is a walk-around inspection of the aircraft. External and internal areas and zones are checked to assure continued airworthiness of the aircraft's power plant, systems, components, and structures. A check compliance interval is 250 FH.

B check's level of inspection is considerably higher than that of the A check. More areas and zones are inspected for integrity. In addition to the A check, B check includes lubrication of systems and components for serviceability of the aircraft. B check compliance interval is 500 FH.

C check is a comprehensive inspection of installations with maximum access to components and systems in various zones. Qualitative and quantitative checks are performed on the components and systems to detect any deterioration. C check compliance interval is 3,000 FH.

D check is a major maintenance check consisting of the following tasks:
- A, B, and C checks.
- Complete corrosion prevention and control of aircraft fuselage, flight control surfaces, wings, landing gear, and empennage.
- External and internal inspection of selected structural items.
- Complete aircraft depainting and repainting.
- Complete aircraft interior refurbishment.
- Aircraft weighing.

D check compliance interval is six years.

7. Alexandra Seno, "Management—Employees First," *AsiaWeek,* October 8, 1999. http://global.factiva.com/en/arch (accessed on 12/10/02).

8. "Gabay" translates literally to "shepherd."

9. Seno, "Management—Employees First."

10. All Saints' Day is an important Philippine holiday observed on November 1 and derived from the Catholic faith of honoring the dead. The day is a Christian holy day that honors all saints of the church, even those not known by name. Roman Catholics are required to attend mass and "refrain from all servile work" on this day.

11. Seno, "Management—Employees First."

CHAPTER 10

The Case of Martha Stewart Living Omnimedia

by Gerry Yemen with Erika H. James and Lynn Perry Wooten

Commentary
by Erika H. James

MARTHA STEWART, FOUNDER and former CEO of Martha Stewart Living Omnimedia (MSO), spent 15 years earning her title as media baroness. By January 2004, the 60-year-old Stewart faced the possibility of spending the same number of years in a federal prison or on probation. The government was investigating Stewart's actions over the sale of her ImClone stocks late in 2001, one day before the Food and Drug Administration rejected the biotechnology company's cancer drug. Stewart was met with four legal actions alleging she breached her fiduciary duties to MSO when she made "materially false and misleading statements" about her involvement in trading ImClone stock.

A comparison of Stewart's statement to MSO shareholders in the firm's annual reports in 2001 and 2002 revealed a sharp contrast:

> Martha Stewart Living Omnimedia (MSO) had another outstanding year in 2001. Despite the difficult economy, we achieved record revenues; record earnings before interest, taxes, depreciation, and amortization (EBITDA); and record earnings per share. We made great progress in further establishing a strong foundation for our future growth.[1]

> 2002 was an extremely difficult and challenging year for Martha Stewart Living Omnimedia. Our year-end financial results reflected both the substantial negative impact of the ongoing government investigations relating to my personal sale of non-Company stock and the generally unfavorable economic environment of the past year.[2]

Although Stewart's firm was not accused of any crime, both her brand and her face were displayed in the media alongside corporate villains from Enron and WorldCom. According to Stewart, "One doesn't anticipate a disaster like this."[3] But now that disaster had struck, what might she anticipate for herself? For her role at MSO? For the very survival of the company she created? How should Stewart deal with the unwanted media attention and negative attacks that were sure to come? Should she keep quiet and trust that her reputation as the perfect homemaker would prevail, or should she speak out and go on the defensive?

From Model to Media Mogul[4]

Martha Kostyra and her five brothers and sisters grew up in Nutley, New Jersey, where her father sold pharmaceuticals and her mother taught school. Her parents and next-door neighbors, who were retired bakers, made sure that she was trained in the traditional female skills: cooking and cleaning. Kostyra was a good student and earned a partial scholarship to Barnard College in New York City. She subsidized her education with modeling. After her sophomore year, Kostyra met and married Andrew Stewart, a law student. Following graduation, Martha Stewart landed several modeling jobs in television commercials for companies like Breck, Clairol, Lifebuoy soap, and Tareyton cigarettes.

Stewart quit modeling in 1965, when her daughter Alexis was born, and began her second career as a stockbroker two years later. Stewart left her Wall Street position during the 1973 recession, and the young family moved to Westport,

Connecticut. Her husband founded a publishing house, while she got busy restoring an 1805 farmhouse called Turkey Hill Farm.[5] In 1976, Stewart started a catering business—The Uncatered Affair—and formed her first partnership with a college friend. Their success was built on an unusual approach that presented food with an artist's eye for design. For ten years they ran the business out of Stewart's basement, and the enterprise grew to generate revenues of $1 million. During the same time, Stewart also opened a retail specialty store in Westport to sell some of the many items she encouraged others to create and use.

By the 1980s, Stewart was also becoming quite accomplished in the writing world: she wrote articles for the *New York Times,* was contributing editor for *Family Circle,* and editor for *House Beautiful. Entertaining,* Stewart's first book, was published in 1982 and was followed by numerous videotapes, dinner music CDs, television appearances—some quite regularly, like *The Today Show*—and eventually many more books. Six years later, Stewart syndicated her own television show, *Martha Stewart Living.* She also entered the consulting world when K-Mart hired her as a "life-style consultant" in 1986. Stewart's world continued to grow when Time Warner financed *Martha Stewart Living* magazine in 1990. Although Stewart had many accomplishments under her belt, her success was not always gracefully received. Two of her neighbors indicated their feelings when they published a smarmy magazine in 1994 called, *Is Martha Stewart Living?* This publication on unstylish living reported on clogged sinks and dead blooms, and featured a cigar-smoking Martha Stewart look-alike.

Despite the popularity of *Martha Stewart Living* magazine, Time Warner was uninterested in financing Stewart's expansion into other media.[6] So in 1997, Stewart used some creative financing and cobbled together enough cash to buy out Time Warner. Although figures were not disclosed, and AOL Time Warner retained 2.5 percent ownership, estimates were between $53.3 to $85 million.[7]

As Stewart's wealth and business acumen grew, *Forbes Magazine* listed her among the wealthiest 400 Americans in 2000. In March 2002, Stewart was nominated and elected to be on the board of directors of the New York Stock Exchange for a two-year term.

Four Business Segments

By 2003, Stewart had built MSO into a thriving media business that employed 580 people in four areas: publishing, television, merchandising, and Internet/direct commerce. The publishing division consisted largely of *Martha Stewart Living,* with a circulation of 250,000; her books with the same title but themed toward special occasions like weddings and holiday seasons; and the "Ask Martha" newspaper column and radio call-in show. The "Ask Martha" program aired on 330 radio stations, covering 91 percent of the United States, and the newspaper column was syndicated in over 200 newspapers nationwide.[8]

Television played a significant role in MSO with the daily *Martha Stewart Living* syndicated program, which had won eight daytime Emmy Awards by 2003. The show also served as a commercial, with frequent showcasing of other MSO products. New shows were also introduced that year that focused on Stewart's garden and her home—no longer just her kitchen.

The merchandising arm of MSO consisted of the Martha Stewart Everyday consumer products in several lines, like home, garden, kitchen, storage, holiday, and paint colors. Sales of these products in 2002 reached nearly $1.5 billion; these were sold through retail partners K-Mart and Zellers (a Canadian company). Stewart expanded the Canadian market in 2003 with product introduction into Sears Canada.

By 2003 catalog distribution was scaled back, with a smaller and more brand-focused assortment of selected products. More emphasis was placed on the Internet site, marthastewart.com, to connect consumers to MSO products and services. The 2002 annual report claimed that the Internet offered future growth potential and had bolstered magazine sales in particular.

Each segment of the company generated revenues from different sources, like merchandise, subscriptions, advertising dollars, and syndicated daily programs. Wall Street analysts liked the company and announced "Good Things Are Happening"[9] in their reports, while the company maintained an "outperform" rating each quarter until the end of June 2002. After the insider trading accusations, analysts gave the company a "hold;" MSO then dropped to the rarely given rank of "underperform." By 2003, despite the negative publicity, Stewart's household products were selling better than her magazines and television shows—up 5 percent from the year before.[10]

June Bugs in the Salad

On June 6, 2002, the first reports surfaced of a Congressional investigation into Stewart's sale of 3,928 shares of ImClone stock nearly six months earlier. MSO stock prices started a long spiral downward with the news of possible insider trading charges. Stewart had developed a business and personal relationship with her broker, Peter Bacanovic, who worked for Merrill Lynch. The initial sales of MSO stock to friends and employees went through him. Her relationship with Bacanovic grew out of her daughter's association with Sam Waksal, CEO of ImClone.[11] Alexis Stewart and

Sam Waksal were featured as a couple in front of a well-decorated Christmas tree in Stewart's 1989 *Holiday Cookbook*.[12]

Waksal's company had been working on a cancer treatment drug when he learned that the Food and Drug Administration was not going to approve the drug for human consumption. Stewart claimed she talked to Bacanovic and sold her nearly 4,000 shares of ImClone on December 27, 2001. On December 28, 2001, the FDA announced they would not review Erbitux (the drug treatment), and ImClone stocks started to tumble. Both Bacanovic and Stewart said they had a prearranged agreement that he was to sell ImClone stock if it dropped below $60 per share. What became part of the legal question over insider trading was whether or not the order existed before December 27, 2001. The story became even more intriguing when Bacanovic's assistant, Douglas Faneuil, told prosecutors that he had talked to Stewart and executed the sale of her shares, since Bacanovic was not in the office when she called. Journalists also reported that Stewart phoned Sam Waksal that same day, but he failed to return her call.

Stewart's very first public comments were made on June 25, 2002, on CBS's *The Early Show* during her weekly cooking segment. The piece looked like an ambush when Jane Clayson, one of the program's anchors, introduced Stewart as her good friend who was fighting allegations of insider trading. The opening shots showed still pictures of Stewart that included one with Stewart and Bacanovic, who appeared to be arm in arm. Then with the camera focused on Clayson, viewers heard what was assumed to be Stewart in the background chopping cabbage. Clayson laid out the entire story and accusations, introduced Stewart, and then addressed Stewart live, saying it was good to see her.

In her first reaction to media probing, Stewart dodged questions from Clayson and said "As you understand, I'm involved in an investigation that has very serious implications. . . . I'm just not at liberty at this time to make any comments whatsoever."[13] She continued to chop cabbage when the camera panned her way, and Stewart commented, "Well I'm here to make salad." Clayson wouldn't let Stewart dismiss the issue that easily and pressed ahead, saying, "We are, but first let me ask you a few things about it." She then continued to ask Stewart about the allegations. Stewart only stopped hacking away at the cabbage briefly as she commented. In a well-spoken manner Stewart explained that the investigation was into the company ImClone and that many other people had also been involved. She said, "Well again, I have nothing to say on the matter." Much to Stewart's frustration, Clayson continued to question her about the affair. After admitting to her involvement in an investigation, a visibly disturbed Stewart finally claimed, "I think this will all be resolved in the near future, and I will be exonerated from this ridiculousness."[14] Refusing to accept Stewart's reluctance to talk about the topic, Clayson pushed on with questions. Finally Stewart said:

> We have been the center of media. . . . I'm in the media business, that's why our company is called Martha Stewart Living Omnimedia, and I have been the subject of very favorable reporting and very unfavorable reporting throughout the years; this is not new to me. And I choose to go ahead with my work, go ahead to concentrate on the good work our company does; my employees and I are hard at work making our company the best omnimedia company in the world, Jane. We will continue to do that, and I want to focus on my salad because that's why we're here.[15]

Adding Ingredients

Sam Waksal was arrested on bank fraud charges related to the ImClone situation on June 12, 2002, a week before Stewart's public comments. Faneuil, who had executed the order to sell Stewart's ImClone shares, pled guilty to a misdemeanor charge of receiving money and other valuables from his boss, Bacanovic, for keeping quiet on what he knew about Stewart's stock sales. On October 12, 2002, Waksal admitted guilt for six counts of bank fraud, securities fraud, conspiracy to obstruct justice, and perjury.

As the stories unfolded, so did the parties claiming injury. A Consolidated and Amended Class Action Complaint was filed on February 3, 2003, in the United States District Court for the Southern District of New York, over Stewart's sale of ImClone stock. The claims of the consolidated suit alleged that Stewart and seven MSO officers misled plaintiffs with statements that were materially false or misleading. As a result, the plaintiffs charged that the market price of the company's stock was inflated and then "dropped after the alleged falsity of the statements became public."[16] Waksal was sentenced to 87 months (seven years) in prison and fined $3 million on June 10, 2003, for his insider trading role and other charges of obstructing justice, perjury, and tax evasion. Faneuil and Bacanovic were both fired from Merrill Lynch, and Faneuil pleaded guilty to a misdemeanor charge for taking gifts in exchange for silence on Stewart's ImClone share sales.

Mixing It Up

Many were delighted to learn of Stewart's fall from grace. She was jeered with headlines like "Martha's Mess," "Cell, Sweet Cell: Martha's Touch Needed,"[17] and suggestions for new television decorating programs called, "From Martha's Cell."[18] Blog sites continued dialogs asking for comments, with bylines like "Martha Stewart and Cover-Ups."[19] Stewart resigned from the NYSE board of directors on October 2, 2002. Continuing the pattern, she gave up her role as chair and CEO of MSO on June 4, 2003, but remained on the company's board—a move she called strategic, "to get the company away from the scandal."[20] She took a new position called chief creative officer (CCO) and still owned 61 percent of the company's stock.

The steps to distance Stewart from MSO were not entirely new, since the 1999 company prospectus had recommended the strategy change.[21] And Stewart's image had disappeared from the *Martha Stewart Living* magazine cover after the December 2000 issue.

The Dressing

Almost a year and a half after Martha Stewart's first public comments on CBS about the ImClone allegations, Stewart took to the airwaves again to discuss her troubles. This time, reporter Barbara Walters interviewed Stewart for ABC's *20/20* show. The entire program was devoted to Stewart's story. Whether the interview helped or hurt Stewart's cause was a matter of public debate, but she was able to get some of her message out. She also confessed, "One doesn't anticipate a disaster like this."[22]

Stewart focused on two points. First, she revealed the dollar amount of her gain from selling ImClone shares—approximately $40,000. According to Stewart, this sum was about .006 percent of her net worth at the time. She said, "It seemed like a tremendous amount of attention focused on one particular person, when indeed on December 27 more than seven million shares of ImClone were traded—I sold 3,900."[23] And Stewart attempted to make a clear distinction between her personal problems and the corporation. When Walters lumped Stewart in with the likes of Enron and WorldCom, Stewart was quick to respond: "We are in a difficult time in corporate America. Business is under great scrutiny—and that something involving my personal life has become a focus of my corporate life is wrong and unfair."[24] At the end of the interview Walters and Stewart agreed that Stewart's mantra, "It's a good thing," had been turned on its head.

Dinner Is Served

Martha Stewart was convicted on March 5, 2004, of obstruction of justice, false statements, and conspiracy to obstruct justice for covering up details about her sale of ImClone stock in 2001. The judge had dismissed the more serious charge of securities fraud on February 27, 2004. Stewart immediately resigned as a board member for Revlon Consumer Products Corporation and over a week later, on March 15, 2004, she stepped down as director and chief creative officer of MSO. Her new title was chief creative consultant. On July 16, 2004, Stewart was sentenced to five months in prison, five months of house arrest, and two years of probation, and was fined $30,000.

The MSO 2003 annual report, like the 2002 annual report, continued to reflect concern over Stewart's legal struggles. For example, revenue in the publishing arm of MSO declined more than 25 percent during the year marked by the scandal. Sharon L. Patrick, president and CEO, said: "We are pleased that fourth quarter results are better than expected. Nevertheless, we continued to feel the negative impact of the events surrounding Martha Stewart's personal legal situation."[25]

With the trial over, Stewart, the company, and consumers waited to see how the conviction would affect MSO. With the company so closely tied to the Martha Stewart brand, would business go forward without her? People didn't necessarily buy Martha Stewart sheets because they were the best out there but because she had given them her seal of approval. Would the present course of keeping Stewart's "legal situation" out of the company finally win out in the marketplace? Was the crisis ending?

Recipe for Survival

Following her initial public reaction, which failed to present a strong message, Stewart hired a crisis-management firm, Citigate Sard Verbinnen, in the summer of 2003. The firm's strategy included hiring all her advisers from outside the company. She also started her own Web site, Marthtalks, to keep her fans, and the generally curious, informed. Her site gave visitors an opportunity to e-mail Stewart personally, a chance to read "notes to Martha," a section with generally favorable news and editorials, and trial updates. On the day of her sentencing, Stewart posted an announcement that her legal experts had appealed the decision, and she vowed to clear her name.[26] Throughout the trial, Stewart's legal team, public relations consultants, and colleagues tried to keep Stewart's legal issues separate from the business.

When Stewart's sentence was handed down on July 16, 2004, the judge issued a "stay," which meant that she stayed out of jail until her appeal process was complete. After sentencing, Stewart expressed regret on her Web site and thanked supporters for the 170,000 e-mails of encouragement. On the courthouse steps, she called the sentencing day "shameful" and said, "What was a small personal matter became, over the last two years, an almost-fatal circus of unprecedented proportion."[27]

Stewart continued to struggle to keep her message from being misunderstood. On a pretaped video interview for the news show *20/20* that aired the Friday after her sentencing, Stewart said, "There are many, many good people who have gone to prison . . . look at Nelson Mandela."[28] On *Larry King Live* a few days later, Stewart clarified her comment, saying, "I am not comparing myself to Nelson Mandela. I am not a Nobel Prize winner."[29]

A core of fans continued to fight for Stewart, using their Web site savemartha.com to get their message out. The group offered downloadable bumper stickers asking the president, and his 2004 opponent, to "pardon Martha." They circulated a petition asking for a presidential pardon (at the time this case was written 18,698 signatures had been collected). Further, fans could purchase aprons, t-shirts, coffee mugs, and hats with slogans like "Free Martha," "Save Martha," and "Pardon Martha."

Effects on the Business

By 2004, Stewart's previously thriving publishing division, mainly the *Martha Stewart Living* magazine, ran 35 percent fewer advertising pages and had lost one-fifth of its subscribers.[30] In spite of the downturn, the firm introduced a new publication, *Everyday Food*. The catalog and Internet advertising revenues fell from $13.7 to $9.4 million between 2002 and 2003.

After the guilty verdict, Viacom quickly pulled Stewart's syndicated program, *Martha Stewart Living,* off the airwaves. Although the program had moved from a popular daytime position to a slot in the middle of the night, it was still running throughout Stewart's trial. Perhaps seeing the writing on the wall, MSO shifted attention toward new programming with the debut of *Petkeeping* with television personality and pet shop owner Marc Morrone a few weeks before. Another new program, *Everyday Food,* was scheduled to debut on PBS stations in January 2005.

The merchandising arm of MSO made money throughout the scandal. Sales for this arm of the firm, with 85 percent of revenue made through K-Mart, nearly doubled in the fourth quarter of 2003.[31] In contrast to brick and mortar sales, on August 3, 2004, MSO announced it would shut down the Internet-direct commerce business (except the floral division) by the end of the year.

Although the company—and Stewart—attempted to keep her personal affairs out of the business, the task was daunting and not necessarily 100 percent effective. After the verdict, MSO stock prices plunged 23 percent. Were these financial problems just bumps in the road for MSO? Would Stewart make a comeback? She created a good brand and product line—should her image be "back up front and center"?

Commentary

The scandal surrounding Martha Stewart had enormous implications for her personally and for MSO. Reputation concerns, branding issues, and business recovery considerations would need to be central components of the crisis management plan. Moreover, the severity of the crisis for MSO was exacerbated by the fact that it was both a sudden and smoldering crisis, suggesting the need to respond to the crisis in multiple ways. The sudden nature of the situation that MSO faced is represented by the absence of information or signals that the company had done anything wrong. In fact, had it not been for the actions of its leader, in a matter of personal affairs, MSO would not have been in a crisis at all. Critical stakeholders, including other leaders at MSO, employees, customers, and even fans of Stewart herself, were unlikely to have been aware of the allegations of financial impropriety in Martha Stewart's personal affairs until they were made public. In that regard, there was no way for the organization to have prepared for the onslaught of negative media attention directed at Martha Stewart and, by extension, at MSO.

Before the allegations became public, however, there may have been signs that the strategic design of MSO would leave the organization vulnerable to and weakened by negative attention of this sort. Specifically, by having the MSO brand so closely aligned with Stewart, the company faced the risk of any adversity that Stewart herself might endure. As Lynn Wooten describes in chapter eight, organizations adopt business strategies to achieve goals that will create value for stakeholders. Clearly, one strategic objective of MSO was to capitalize on the attention generated by its founder and leader, Martha Stewart. The goal was to build a loyal customer base by urging customers to identify with the homemaking queen and put trust in her company's products. Such a strategy is most advantageous when the public overwhelmingly adores a company's leader. Stewart, however, generated as much if not more negative attention as she did positive attention. Thus, Stewart's actions reinforced her already tarnished image, which, in turn, had negative implications for MSO.

The challenge for companies is to assess the risk of closely identifying with a celebrity. As firms like Nike can attest, there are clear financial gains to be had from such partnerships. Consider, for example, Nike's longstanding and extremely lucrative arrangements with sports legends Michael Jordan and Tiger Woods. However, with big rewards comes the potential for big losses in both firm reputation and revenues when a celebrity partner is tainted. MSO took a gamble by so closely identifying its image with that of its celebrity founder. Unfortunately, the company has suffered the consequences.

A Panic Situation. Particularly relevant to the situation faced by Stewart and MSO is the notion of panic, as Mary Waller discusses in chapter six. If, as Waller describes, panic is a state of being that follows fear, then we are perfectly positioned to understand the reasons for Stewart's behavior and communication following the publicity of the allegations against her. Clearly Stewart was experiencing fear. Her personal reputation, her career, and her media empire were under threat. An initial response to threat is to flee from it. Literally fleeing from the threat was not an option for Stewart, but she did attempt to escape or distance herself from the situation. Her public communications not only centered on denial rhetoric but also could be interpreted as her attempt to downplay the seriousness of the allegations. Furthermore, in an obvious attempt to protect her company, Stewart, on numerous public occasions, attempted to separate her own troubles from those of MSO.

In addition to the attempts to flee from threat, Waller points out that panic induces a need to control threatening situations, to somehow direct or manage the ambiguity associated with the crisis. Typically, control-based responses to threat tend to be rigid, with key decision makers displaying an inflexibility that is antithetical to the leadership qualities the contributors to this book advocate. One noticeable example of Stewart's attempt to control her situation was her engagement with the media. Continuing to respond to or engage with media inquiries is exactly what someone in her position should do. But the content and manner of her engagement were problematic. Take, for example, the television episode on *The Early Show* with reporter Jane Clayson. One hopes that Stewart had expected Clayson to inquire about the investigation of her financial and legal troubles, and that Stewart would have been prepared with a message that both respected the sensitivity of the investigation *and* satisfied some of her critical stakeholders. Instead, it seemed that Stewart succumbed to panic during the interview; her only way out was an attempt to control the interview by redirecting it to the making of her salad. To the public, her comments seemed ridiculous, and her overall performance as a leader, much less a crisis leader, was further called into question.

For Stewart and for MSO, the issue of panic, or panic management, is best addressed in the rhetoric that was offered in response to and throughout the crisis situation. Stewart was heavily criticized for her perceived lack of humility and her failure to demonstrate ownership or responsibility for her situation. This is not uncommon. To be clear, an expression of responsibility is not the same as a guilty plea, but it does convey to stakeholders an understanding that crises such as the one

Stewart faced are not completely externally driven. In failing to acknowledge that, MSO paid a price.

Strategic Communication. So what could Stewart have done differently to protect her own reputation and that of MSO? According to David Wooten's discussion of apologies in chapter five, at the very least Stewart should have communicated in a slightly more apologetic tone. Doing so would have helped shape how the public, and MSO consumers in particular, felt about Stewart. Moreover, they might have found it easier to sympathize with her. An apology that conveyed regret, acknowledged at least some aspect of Stewart's responsibility in the crisis, and committed to more responsible behavior in the future would have been the display of a key crisis leadership competency, as I describe in chapter three. In particular, an apology can go a long way toward demonstrating that one is taking ownership of the decision-making process during a crisis. In addition, a more apologetic communication may have been especially helpful in Stewart's case in light of her already precarious reputation.

In thinking about the role of rhetoric in the Stewart case, Timothy Coombs's chapter on situational crisis communication theory (SCCT) is relevant in that it speaks to the strategic role that rhetoric or communication can play. Recall that SCCT, and the communication strategies it suggests, is motivated by the type and the extent of the reputational threat a crisis poses. According to Coombs, both marketing and psychological research suggest that stakeholders will attribute the cause of the crisis to either the organization (or its representatives) or to external factors. The more fault is attributed to the organization, the more potential harm to the firm's reputation. MSO clearly bore a great deal of the burden of Stewart's personal troubles. Identifying the specific nature or type of crisis would have been an important first step in the company's response.

To use Coombs's terminology, one could argue that the situation faced by MSO represents a victim crisis, meaning that the organization suffered harm as a result of outside forces rather than its own actions. In this case, MSO suffered largely because of the personal dealings of its leader, not because the company itself did anything wrong. Yet, given the strong association between Stewart and MSO, it is unlikely that the public would have distinguished the firm from her. This is evidenced by MSO's declining revenue and stock price during Stewart's investigation. And because the public is perhaps less able to disentangle Stewart from MSO, communication strategies appropriate for a victim crisis may be unsuitable in this instance. More relevant may be communication strategies in response to preventable crises, or those crises in which an organizational member or members knowingly put stakeholders at risk. Coombs argues that such crises generate strong attributions of responsibility and therefore are a large threat to an organization's reputation. In applying SCCT to the situation facing MSO, Stewart and other crisis leaders should have also considered the factors that were likely to have influenced the public's perception during the crisis. Clearly, Stewart's tenuous public persona and reputation should have been an important consideration.

In selecting the most appropriate communication response, SCCT suggests that communication that attempts to "rebuild" will likely be most effective. In the situation faced by Stewart and MSO, the objective should have been to rebuild reputation and brand image. Like Wooten, Coombs argues that rhetoric acknowledging responsibility will be perceived most positively and will be most likely to influence the perceptions of others. Unfortunately, Stewart adopted a more denial-based posture, which failed to line up with the type of crisis she and her company faced. In sum, although crisis leadership encompasses a variety of skills and competencies, how and what one communicates during a crisis is a critical element of successful crisis leadership.

1. Martha Stewart Living Omnimedia Annual Report, 2001. http://ccbn5.mobular.net/ccbn/7/55/59/ (accessed on January 9, 2004).

2. Martha Stewart Living Omnimedia Annual Report, 2002. http://ccbn22.mobular.net/ccbn/7/206/214/ (accessed on January 9, 2004).

3. "Profile Martha Stewart," ABC *20/20,* September 7, 2003.

4. Most of the information in the first two paragraphs was based on an interview with Martha Stewart on June 2, 1995, in Williamsburg, Virginia. http://www.achievement.org/autodoc/page/ste0bio-1?rand=674 (accessed on October 1, 2003).

5. At the time this case was written, Martha Stewart still lived in the farmhouse that she featured in many of her books, magazine pieces, and television shows.

6. Todd Eberle, "Empire by Martha," *Vanity Fair* (September 2001): 398.

7. Ibid.

8. Martha Stewart Living Omnimedia Annual Report, 2001. http://ccbn5.mobular.net/ccbn/7/55/59/ (accessed on January 9, 2004).

9. Douglas M. Arthur and Mary Meeker, "Martha Stewart Living," Morgan Stanley Dean Witter, August 23, 2000.

10. Naomi Aoki, "Polishing the Sheen on a Tarnished Image. With the Jury Out on Her Celebrity Selling Power, Jordan's Ads Tout Martha Stewart," *Boston Globe,* September 11, 2003, E 1.

11. Art Guart and John Lehmann, "Sam a Pet to Martha," *New York Post,* October 8, 2003. http://www.nypost.com/ news/nationalnews/58793.htm (accessed December 4, 2003).

12. Ibid.

13. "Marketing Martha, Post Crisis," CBS News, June 4, 2003. http://www.cbsnews.com/stories/2003/06/04/ eveningnews/main557018.shtml (accessed on June 9, 2003).

14. Stewart later referred to this response as an "unfortunate choice of words."

15. At the time this case was written, viewers could go to http://www.cbsnews.com/stories/2003/06/04/ eveningnews/main557018.shtml to see the footage.

16. Martha Stewart Living Omnimedia Annual Report, 2002: 10.

17. John Kelso, Friday, June 6, 2003. http://talkshows.about.com/gi/dynamic/ offsite.htm?site=http%3A%2F%2Fwww.statesman.com%2Fmetrostate%2Fcontent%2Fmetro%2Fkelso%2F0603%2F060603.html.

18. Fabio Luss, http://talkshows.about.com/gi/dynamic/ offsite.htm?site=http%3A%2F%2Fwww.truedorktimes.com%2F0902%2Fmarthainjail.htm.

19. The Yin Blog, http://yin.blog-city.com/read/97071.htm.

20. "Profile Martha Stewart," *20/20.*

21. Constance L. Hays and Tracie Rozhon, "Is There Life for Martha Stewart Living Omnimedia without Martha?" *New York Times,* September 5, 2002, C-5.

22. "Profile Martha Stewart," *20/20.*

23. Ibid.

24. Ibid.

25. Martha Stewart Living Omnimedia Annual Report, 2001. http://premium.hoovers.com/subscribe/co/ secoutline.xhtml?COID=53053&ipage=2645893 (accessed on March 9, 2004).

26. At the time this case was written, readers could view the Web site at: http://www.marthatalks.com/.

27. Krysten Crawford, "Martha: I cheated no one," CNNMoney. http://cnnmoney.printthis.clickability.com/pt/ cpt?action=cpt&title+Martha+Steawart+gets+fincance (accessed on September 1, 2004).

28. Ibid.

29. Ibid.

30. Daniel Kadlec, "Not A Good Thing for Martha: A Lie Turned Her into a Convicted Felon. How a Woman Known for Perfection Made Mistakes at Almost Every Turn." *Time* (March 15, 2004). http://global.factiva.com/ en/arch/print_results.asp (accessed on March 9, 2004).

31. Ibid., 5.